SUBJECTIVE EVOLUTION
OF CONSCIOUSNESS

All Glories to Śrī Guru and Gauranga

SUBJECTIVE EVOLUTION OF CONSCIOUSNESS

The Play of the Sweet Absolute

His Divine Grace

SWAMI B. R. SRIDHAR

SRI CHAITANYA SARASWAT MATH

Published by Vaishnava Seva Society
P.O. Box 8040
Santa Cruz, California 95061
(831) 462-4712
www.SevaAshram.com

First Printing 1989 3,000 Copies
by Guardian of Devotion Press

Second Printing 1998 2,500 copies
By Ananta Printing and Publishing

Third Printing 2011 5,000 copies
By Giri Print Service for
Sripad Bhakti Madhava Puri Maharaj

Fouth Printing 2018 On Demand
By Vaishnava Seva Society

Edited by Bhakti Sudhir Goswami
and Swami Bhakti Vidhan Mahayogi

Special thanks to all the devotees to helpled in the production of these editions and those whose selfless service and generous contributions made these printings possible.

Contents

Preface

Evolution is generally thought of as something objective. But objective evolution is a misperception of reality. Evolution is actually based on consciousness, which is subjective. Subjective evolution, however, seems to be objective evolution to the ignorant.

In ignorance we think of ourselves as subjects, although in reality the Lord is the subject and we are His objects. We think of ourselves as proprietors although we are His property.

It is said that all things happen by the will of the Vaiṣṇavas, the devotees of the Lord. A Vaiṣṇava is like a faithful employee who speaks the will of the employer; he has no will of his own: the will of the pure Vaiṣṇava is nothing but the will of God. In ignorance, however, we try to make the Lord our servant, but this is like using a *śāla-grāma śilā* to crack nuts. The Lord is not an object. He is the seer, the doer, and the knower – the Supreme Subject – but we foolishly think of ourselves as such.

The concept of subjective evolution is explained in *Śrīmad-Bhāgavatam (10.14.22):*

tasmād idaṁ jagad aśeṣam asat-svarūpaṁ
svapnābham asta-dhiṣaṇaṁ puru-duḥkha-duḥkham

"By an illusion created by the Lord the universe appears to be real, although it is not, just as miseries we suffer in a dream are only imaginary."

Unintelligent people take the subject as an object. It is ignorance to confuse the eye with the seer, or the brain with the knower. This is described in *Śrīmad-Bhāgavatam (1.3.31):*

yathā nabhasi meghaugho
reṇur vā pārthivo 'nile
evaṁ draṣṭari dṛśyatvam
āropitam abuddhibhiḥ

"The unintelligent equate the sky with the clouds, the air with the dust particles floating in it, and think that the sky is cloudy or that the air is dirty."

Consciousness is not a product of the world; the world is a product of consciousness. This world is a perverted reflection of the spiritual world. In the material world, the world of exploitation, as Darwin says, it is a question of survival of the fittest. We must exploit to survive: *jīvo jīvasya jīvanam.* But in the spiritual world, the land of dedication, everyone is a serving unit. There we will find a happy life through dedication.

In that supersubjective realm, Śrī Krishna is eternally engaged in his divine play with his most intimate servitors. And as our consciousness evolves through dedication, we will find our highest prospect there, where we have a part to play in the pastimes of the Sweet Absolute.

President-Āchārya Śrī Chaitanya Sāraswat Maṭh
Śrīla Bhakti Sundar Govinda Dev-Goswāmī Mahārāj

Founder-Āchārya Śrī Chaitanya Sāraswat Maṭh
Śrīla Bhakti Rakṣak Śrīdhar Dev-Goswāmī Mahārāj

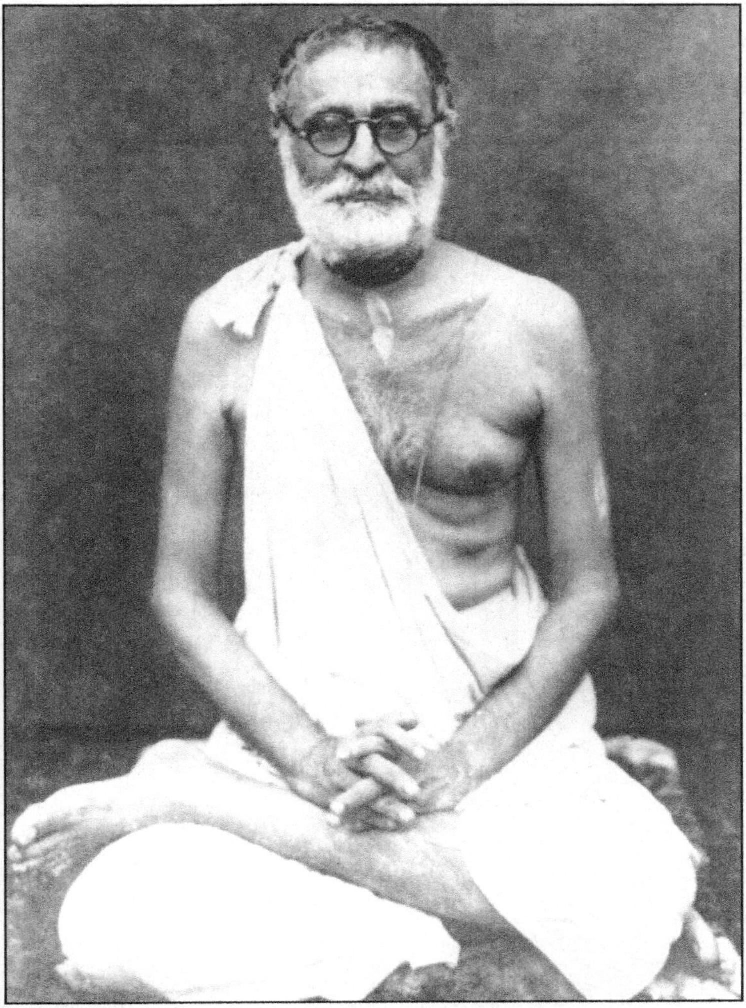

Śrīla Bhaktisiddhānta Saraswatī Ṭhākura

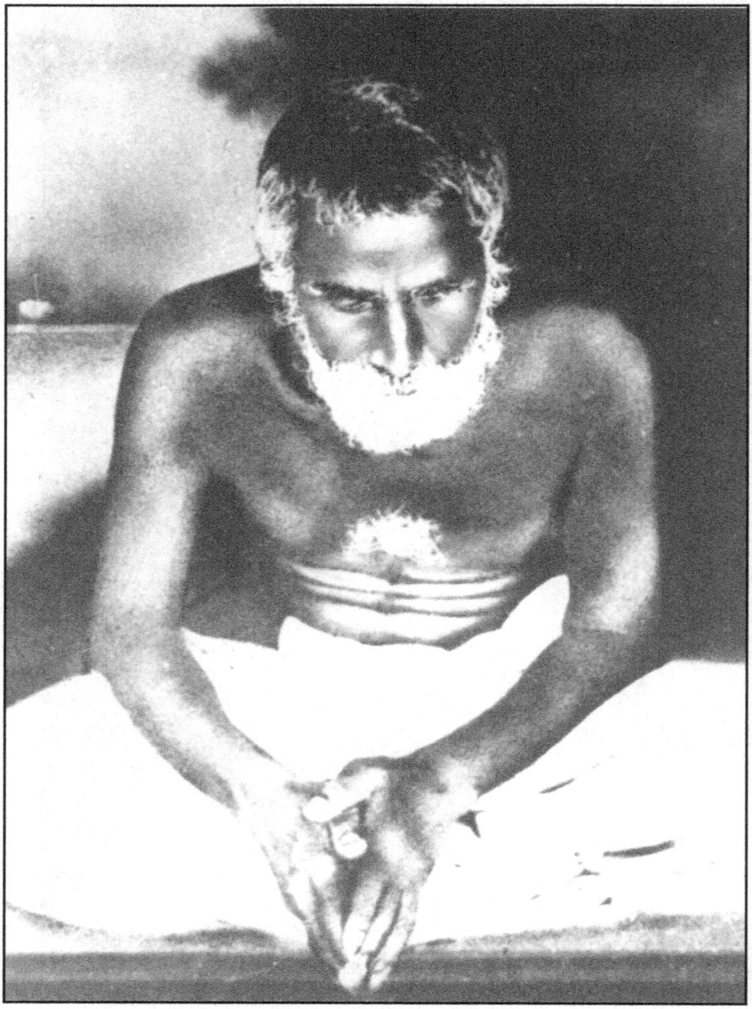

Śrīla Gaura Kiśora Dāsa Bābajī Mahārāj

Śrīla Bhaktivinoda Ṭhākura

Fossilism, Hypnotism, & The Cosmos

This chapter is an excerpt from a conversation between Śrīla Śrīdhar Mahārāj, neurophysiologist Dr. Daniel Murphey and physical organic chemist Dr. Thoudam Singh

Dr. Singh: When scientists speak of evolution they mean that life has evolved from matter. I have heard you speak of evolution with quite a different concept. You say that everything is evolving from consciousness.

Śrīla Śrīdhar Mahārāj: Yes, consciousness comes first and then matter. The basis of all things material is consciousness, which is spiritual. Consciousness can contact consciousness directly. When consciousness comes into the stage of matter, material conception, we experience a kind of vague consciousness; first there is hazy consciousness and then material consciousness. But everything has its spiritual side. And as eternal souls, our direct connection is really only with the conscious aspect of existence. For example, the Earth is conceived of as a woman. According to the *Vedas*, the presiding deity of the Earth is a woman. And the sun is conceived of as a *devata*, a male god.

The soul, coming into material consciousness, must come through some hazy reflection of consciousness, *cidābhāsa*. Only then can the soul experience material consciousness. Before pure consciousness evolves to material consciousness, it will pass through a hazy stage of consciousness or *cidābhāsa*. So in the background of every material thing, there is a spiritual conception. This cannot but be true.

Dr. Singh: What is *cidābhāsa*?

Śrīla Śrīdhar Mahārāj: Something like mind. Suppose consciousness comes to feel matter. When consciousness is coming to the material world to know the material world, it has to first pass through material consciousness, and then it can feel what is matter. According to Darwin's theory, matter gradually produces consciousness, but before producing consciousness it must produce some hazy consciousness, then mind, and then the soul. But in reality, it is just the opposite. So subjective evolution parallels objective or material evolution. But in the evolution of consciousness, the supersubject is first, then the individual soul or *jīva*-subject is next. Then, from the subjective consciousness of the *jīvas*, matter is produced. But consciousness must penetrate hazy consciousness to perceive matter.

I say that the process of evolution moves from the top downward. The Absolute Reality – if we at all assert that there is anything which is the absolute reality – must possess two qualifications. What is that? First, in the words of Hegel, He must be by Himself: He is his own cause.

Second – and more important to us, He is for Himself: He exists to fulfill His own purpose. He is not subservient to any other entity, for then His position would be secondary. Reality the Absolute is full in Himself. All other things are coming from Him. The perfect substance already exists. What appears to us as imperfect comes down according to our own defective senses.

The imperfect must be dependent upon the perfect, the ultimate reality. And the imperfect may be so arranged by Him in order to prove His perfection. To prove the perfection of the Absolute, there is conditioned and unconditioned, finite and infinite reality. The defective world therefore has an indirect relation to the truth.

However, consciousness cannot jump at once into the conception of matter; it must pass through a process to come to material consciousness. From the marginal position, from the verge of the higher eternal potency, evolution and dissolution of this material world begins. This takes place only on the outskirts of *svarūpa-śakti*, which is the system responsible for the evolution of the spiritual plane, and is an eternally evolving dynamic whole. It is not that nondifferentiation is the origin of differentiation. An eternally differentiated substance exists. That plane is filled with *līlā*, dynamic pastimes. If a static thing can be conceived of as eternal, then why can't a dynamic thing be conceived of as eternal? That plane of *svarūpa-śakti* is fully evolved within. It is eternal. Evolution and dissolution concern only the degradation of the subtle spirit to the gross material platform and his evolution towards perfection. Here there is evolution and dissolution, but these things do not exist in the eternal abode of *svarūpa-śakti.*

Dr. Singh: Objective evolution is what modern science calls Darwinian evolution, but how does subjective evolution unfold in Krishna conscious science?

Śrīla Śrīdhar Mahārāj: You have to take the example of hypnotism. Through a form of mystic "hypnotism," the supersubject controls the subject to see a particular thing, and he is bound to see that. One may think that as we see a stone, the stone compels us to see it as stone, but it is just the opposite: we are compelled to see it as stone being under the influence of the supersubject who displays everything as He likes. When He commands, "See stone," then we shall see stone. Full control over whatever we see rests in His hands. No power to control what we see rests in the objective world. The objective world is fully controlled by the subjective. This is confirmed in Bhagavad-gītā, where Krishna says *paśya me yogam aiśvaryam*: "If I say, 'Behold my mystic power,' you are bound to see it. You have no other choice."

Krishna says *mattaḥ smṛtir jñānam apohanaṁ ca*: He is the prime cause of remembrance, forgetfulness, and intelligence. He is the controller. For His own pleasure, His *līlā*, He can do anything. This is true not only in the material world, but also in His own domain. What is meant by this statement of the *Gītā* concerns this *brahmānda*, this material world. The gist of this statement is that from the lower planetary systems up to the highest – this entire area of evolution and dissolution – everything is manipulated by Him. No credit can be attached to any external thing. All credit should go to the Center who controls everything.

And reality is subjective. It is based on consciousness. Color is perceived through the eye. It is not that the color is there and the eye can catch it. But the seer sees through the eye and perceives color. So color is a perception. Its position as actual substance should be traced to the subtle plane of existence. This is the nature of reality: the gross is coming from the subtle. In Sāṅkhya philosophy, of course, that is described as a bifurcated thing. According to Sāṅkhya philosophy, there are three branches of reality: the sense, the senses, and the sense objects. Sound is created by the ear, color is produced by the eye, and so on.

The objects of the senses are in the mode of ignorance, *tama-guṇa*, the sensual instruments are in the mode of passion, *rāja-guṇa*, and the power of sensation is in the mode of goodness, *sattva-guṇa*. From these proceed light, the eye, and color; sky, the ear, and sound. In this way, mundane reality branches in three ways: *tama*, *rāja*, and *sattva*. So the gross world is coming from the subtle through the channel of consciousness. The feeler, the instrument of perception, is creating the object of his perception.

Try to understand this principle of hypnotism. The whole thing is hypnotism – this whole creation – and it is completely in the hand of the Supreme Subject. All material laws have no meaning; the laws and the sublaws are all pertaining to the subjective world.

Dr. Murphey: But how can one perceive this sort of hypnotism?

Śrīla Śrīdhara Mahārāja: How can we know beforehand that in a laboratory, combining hydrogen and oxygen – two gases – will produce water? Only when one comes to a particular stage of scientific knowledge can he know that a more subtle thing like gas can produce a tangible material thing like water. In that way, when you have an idea of the higher substance, then you can understand how from the subtle, the gross has originated.

The relative world is a perverted reflection of the absolute reality. Highly qualified things must be given the position of causal importance. It is not that a lower thing can produce a higher thing, but it is easy for a higher thing to produce something lower. This is not difficult to understand.

The modern scientific position is saying basically that stone can produce soul; but why not consider that soul can produce stone? We have to inquire about that process – how the soul can produce stone. But we have done away with that and instead we say that stone is gradually producing soul – we are very fond of investigating in that line. Why? The subtle should be given more importance than the gross. Why should we think that man has created God, and not that God has created man?

Dr. Singh: Then God is the magician and we are His subjects?

Śrīla Śrīdhar Mahārāj: Not only is He a magician, but

the Super-magician. He is not merely the kind of magician that is within our experience.

The modern scientific position is saying basically that stone can produce soul; but why not consider that soul can produce stone?

Dr. Murphey: What is the role of *Yogamāyā*, the Lord's internal potency?

Śrīla Śrīdhar Mahārāj: She is found in the eternal company of Krishna. In our conception of divinity, *puruṣa/prakṛti*, the masculine/feminine, are existing together. Potent and potency, substance and potency, are inconceivably interconnected. Otherwise, if we conceive of the Supreme Soul as existing independent of any potency, that will be the *brahman* conception of Śaṇkarācarya: ultimate consciousness as non-differentiated oneness. So the Absolute Truth includes both potent and potency – *puruṣa/prakṛti* – consciousness with energy.

Actually there are three main elements to be traced within divinity: *jñāna, bala*, and *krīya.* The eternal aspect of the absolute whole is divided in three ways: energy, consciousness, and ecstasy. Thinking, willing and feeling. *Sat, cit, ānanda. Sat,* the potency for maintaining existence, is the potency of Baladeva (*bala*). *Cit*, the aspect of consciousness, is Vāsudeva (*jñāna*). And *ānanda*, ecstatic feeling, is Rādhikā (*kriya*). *Jñāna, bala, krīya* (knowledge, strength, feeling); *sat, cit, ānanda* (eternity, cognition, bliss); *sandhīnī, samvīt, hlādinī* (existence, realization, ecstasy): Baladeva, Krishna, Rādhārānī. These are the three phases of *advaya-jñāna*, or the one whole. The one whole can be thought of in its primary, evolved stage in three ways: main consciousness, main energy, and main satisfaction. In three phases we are to conceive of that ultimate reality. It is there: *jñāna, bala, krīya ca*. Thinking, feeling, willing. *Sat, cit, ānanda. Satyam, śivam, sundaram* (eternity, auspiciousness, beauty). And these three principles are expressed through evolution and dissolution in the eternal and non-eternal.

These aspects of theism have been dealt with in a very scientific way in the *Śrī Kṛṣṇa Saṁhitā* of Bhaktivinoda Ṭhākura. Once, I considered from this point of view the question of the planets in Vedic cosmology. We see that by the movement of the different planets, a solar eclipse is caused by the moon's shadow falling upon the Earth. And yet in the scriptures it has been described that during an eclipse, the planet Rāhu is devouring the sun or the moon. When Śrīla Bhaktisiddhānta Saraswatī Ṭhākura was in Purī during his last days and an eclipse came, one devotee who was supposed to know *siddhānta*, the conclusions of scripture, was sitting next to Prabhupāda. He suddenly ridiculed the idea given in the *Bhāgavatam* that during a solar or lunar eclipse Rāhu devours the sun or moon.

I could not tolerate that such a remark should be passed

in regard to the *Bhāgavatam* and argued that what *Śrīmad-Bhāgavatam* has stated is not to be taken lightly. I offered what seemed like some far-fetched support. I said that in his *Jaiva Dharma*, Bhaktivinoda Ṭhākura has created so many characters, but I think that they are not imaginary. What he has written might have occurred during some other millennium (*kalpa*), or day of Brahmā, and that has now come to the surface. In this way I went on to support the cosmological position of the *Bhāgavatam* by arguing that what is necessary to prove reality must also have some real position. It cannot but be. In this way my argument went and Prabhupāda supported me.

In understanding the position of the planet Rāhu, what Śukadeva and Vyāsadeva have said is geographically impossible, but their statements are there in *Śrīmad-Bhāgavatam*, and the literal meaning of the scriptures is not to be taken lightly. Considering the importance of the literal meaning of scripture, Bhaktivedānta Swāmī Mahārāja presented *Bhagavad-gītā As It Is*. I thought, "How am I to prove what the *Bhāgavatam* says? I don't know. But what is said in Śrīmad-*Bhāgavatam* must be true. I have faith in that."

There are so many statements on the cosmology of the universe in the scriptures. The Aryans, the spiritually developed men of former times, used to see everything as consciousness. They saw that the shadow is also conscious. The shadow, *ābhāsa*, is also considered to be a stage of consciousness. Only through that shadowy stage of consciousness can we come to the material conception of a thing. Before we reach the conception of a shadow, we must pass through some mental stage, and personification may be attached to that mental stage. The personification of the shadow may be referred to as "Rāhu."

The soul approaches matter, the material world, but before that, he must pass through a shadowy stage of consciousness called *cidābhāsa*. Consciousness passes through the shadow level of consciousness into matter, non-consciousness. And that shadow stage of consciousness has its personality. It is also conscious, and may be known as "Rāhu."

Every material conception presupposes a spiritual conception of that particular thing. The shadow through which consciousness must pass in order to perceive things as material has personality, and in the *Bhāgavatam*, the *ṛṣis*, the seers of the truth, are addressing it as Rāhu. Because they are highly developed, they find the personal aspect of existence everywhere. What we perceive to be dead matter, they perceive to be conscious. Therefore, they always take the personal perspective.

The soul, when going to experience any material conception, will have to pass through a medium which influences his consciousness to see things as material. What is concrete matter is unknown. It is a mere effect of consciousness. As everything material must have some conscious origin, or origin in personal consciousness, there must be a personal conception of the sun, the moon, the Earth, and all the planets. Before we reach the conception of a shadow or any other object, the soul has to pass through a conscious stage. That stage has some spiritual existence as a person. Therefore the *Bhāgavatam* refers to the sun, the moon, and the planet Rāhu, as persons. Everything – the Earth, the moon, the stars, the planets – has a personal conception. In the background of what we can perceive with our dull senses, everything that is said to be matter, there must be a personal conception. Without the influence of a personal conception, consciousness cannot reach the stage of gross matter.

Therefore, in the ancient scriptures we find that the great sages and *ṛṣis* are always addressing everything within this world as a person. Although to us it is dead matter, they have considered them as persons. Why? The matter is rather the shadow of the personal entity. The personal, conscious entity is more real, and the matter we perceive through dimmed consciousness is less real.

Dr. Murphey: So that shadow is Rāhu?

Śrīla Śrīdhar Mahārāj: When we conceive of the personal representation of that shadow, it will be known as Rāhu. Everything is conscious. The shadow, its effect – everything. When the moon is between the sun and the Earth, the shadow of the moon is coming here, and what is coming is also conscious. Everything is conscious first – then there is matter. From the personal conception things evolve to gross consciousness. It is all personal. So the *ṛṣis* with such a vision of reality used to address everything as a person: the trees, the mountains, the sun, the moon, the ocean. When pure consciousness is coming to experience pure matter, then there must first be some mixed stage, and that is a person suffering in *karma*. Person means they are not a fully developed spiritual person at present, but in a mixed condition. So what the *ṛṣis* are saying – that everything is a person – is real; it is not a concoction.

Everything is conscious. As the present scientists say everything is matter, we have real cause to think that everything is conscious. Whatever you see does not matter; we can directly feel what is in our nature. That is conscious. Our consciousness may be in a developed or degraded position, but consciousness is nearer to us. We feel our mental energy only.

Dr. Murphey: This is a bit difficult for us to fully grasp. When we see color, what are we actually seeing?

Śrīla Śrīdhar Mahārāj: That is a mental stage.

Dr. Singh: What is the reality of that object?

Śrīla Śrīdhar Mahārāj: Reality – that is in the soul. Only the soul is real; the seer is reality. The subject is real. And whatever the subject feels also emanates from the subject.

Dr. Singh: But are the objects the subject perceives also persons? When we are seeing the color red, now is red also a personality?

Śrīla Śrīdhar Mahārāj: Everything has its representation in the original, personal, conscious, spiritual reality. Otherwise, there is no possibility of its being reflected into this plane as matter. First there is consciousness and then when it is in a more gross condition, it appears to be matter. In the study of ontology it is taught that when studying a particular thing, although we can know that it has certain attributes to the eye, and that it appears to the ear in a particular way, these are all appearances. Independent of appearances, the ontological aspect of a thing – what it is, the reality of a thing – is unknown and unknowable. My contention is that when consciousness is going to feel non-conscious matter it will have to pass through a conscious area to meet the material object. So the full perception of that material thing cannot but be conscious; and consciousness always indicates person. First there is conception and then the material idea.

The conscious world is very near and the material world is very far off. Therefore the great *ṛṣis*, whose thinking is highly developed, address whatever they find within the environment as if they are all persons. In the *Vedas*, the ancient scriptural literature of India, we find that the saints and sages are always in the midst of so many persons; in the background everything is a person.

Dr. Murphey: And person means thinking, feeling, willing.

Śrīla Śrīdhar Mahārāj: Thinking, feeling, willing – a living entity has three phases. And it is also the same with God and his potency. There is a subject existing first, and then his experiences. And experiences of the subtlemost character come first and are given the most importance. And when the subject is coming to the more distant area to conceive of matter, that will be the farthest point from him. He will address everything by which he is surrounded with personal conceptions.

A personal conception cannot but assert that matter is far off. The direct connection of consciousness is with the shadow, the reflection of the material into the conscious world. The soul can understand that only. If matter can exist independently, then also matter has a shadow in the conscious world and the soul is concerned with that shadow.

In other words, there is the person and then the body. Just as the body is the after-effect of the conscious living agent, matter is the after-effect of spirit. Irrespective of all material consciousness, that which is in direct contact with soul is all personal. *Cidābhāsa* is something like the mental substance we have within.

There are two kinds of persons, *kṣara* and *akṣara*: the pure liberated soul and the soul who is struggling in matter. When liberated and non-liberated persons are mixed within the world of material transactions, whether as moving or non-moving entities, or whatever their position might be, still they should be considered persons. Since everything is a unit of consciousness, everything has personal existence.

Dr. Murphey: So externally we see the Ganges as water, but in reality she is a person.

Śrīla Śrīdhar Mahārāj: Everything is a person. Before we go to the material conception, we must pass through the personal conception or aspect of that thing. In Vṛndāvana everything is conscious, but some things are posing in a passive way. But they are all conscious: the Yamunā river, the cows, the trees, the fruit – everything is conscious, spiritual, but they pose in different ways. Being able to detect the conscious characteristic in everything, the Aryans saw all of nature as conscious and personal, and addressed everything as conscious.

Consciousness and personality are the universal basis of reality. Whatever we may experience is conscious. The reflection of a material object is within me, and the plane within me is conscious. The subject is consciousness, and whatever kind of thing the object may be, it casts its reflection into the plane of consciousness. The observer of any objective reality is involved only with consciousness from beginning to end, and can have no conception of matter apart from consciousness.

Dr. Murphey: How can we differentiate consciousness from mind?

Śrīla Śrīdhar Mahārāj: In *Bhagavad-gītā* the path of differentiation between consciousness and mind is suggested: *indriyāṇi parāṇy āhur*. What is *ātmā*, the soul, the spiritual conception? We have come to the world conception by a particular process. By the process of elimination we can trace out what the mind is. It is said that the basis of the mind is acceptance and rejection: *saṅkalpa-vikalpa* – "I want this, I don't want that." What is the mind? A thing that contains apathy and sympathy for the external world. That is the mind. We have to trace within us what that thing is. It is within us, and one has to enter into his own self and try to have some personal experience of what the mind is. Then by internal analysis one can try to come directly in touch with the faculty of judgment, reason, intelligence, by asking, "What is intelligence? Where is it within me?" We should try to find that out and come in touch with that directly. We should inquire, "What is the mind? It is already within me. But what is it? And what is reason within me? What is the source of the mind and intelligence? And crossing the stage of the decisive faculty, what is the soul?" We must try, as a yogi does, to come in direct touch with the elements within us. Mind and intelligence are within each of us. Why should we not be able to trace out exactly what they are, to see internally what they are?

Dr. Murphey: When our faith is growing in a particular direction, how can we know that our realizations are coming from our own internal self, from our inner consciousness, and not from the influence of the environment, the circumstances that surround us?

Śrīla Śrīdhar Mahārāj: The self is in a dormant state, but by some external help it may be reawakened, just as when one is sleeping, by external interference a man can be roused. It is something like that. Someone is dormant, but when, by external help, he awakes from his slumber, he again becomes aware of himself. Once he is awakened and his self-awareness has returned, he immediately knows, "I was such and such; I am such and such." By the help of our friends we may recover our health. In the same way, if we continue to apply the process of *bhakti*, we shall become more and more conscious of our self and of reality. We are our own guarantee.

Dr. Murphey: I wanted to clarify one point. In Kapila's system of analysis, Śāṅkhya, he says that *pradhāna* is "that unmanifested matter which is eternal." You say that everything is consciousness. Is *pradhāna* also composed of consciousness?

Śrīla Śrīdhar Mahārāj: Yes. What is material is only the misconception which is the cause of all this material existence. But it also has personality – Devī, the goddess.

The world begins within misconception. When you have the proper conception, then you can read Krishna *līlā* everywhere. Everything will excite you about Vṛndāvana. You won't see the outward thing if you are relieved from misconception. A madman has a maladjusted brain. He may be in the midst of friends, but he is lost in his madness, his paranoia. When he goes back to his normal position, he finds the same thing – all friends. In the same way, everything is all right – only the disease, our misconception needs to be removed.

Dr. Murphey: The disease is our lack of Krishna consciousness.

Śrīla Śrīdhar Mahārāj: Lack of consciousness means misconception, disease. This is described in *Śrīmad-Bhāgavatam: bhayaṁ dvitīyābhinivesataḥ syād* – the disease is separate interest. The deviation from our normal spiritual condition, the development of misconception, is based on the charm – the prospect – of separate interest. That is the root cause of all misunderstanding. The conception of local, provincial interest has caused the difference between a proper conception of reality and misconception. We have gone away from the central conception. From universal consciousness we have come to this provincial plane. And according to the gradation of consciousness in its development from provincial to universal, we may find ourselves in so many different planets or planes of existence: *bhūr, bhuvaḥ, svāh, jana, mahār, tapa, satya*, all these different stages of development are involved in this process of provincialism and universalism. But loss of consciousness of the center is the root of this entire material existence.

One who is conscious of the organic whole, on the other hand, is in the most healthy position. That is proper adjustment, and maladjustment is the cause of our present diseased condition. Adjustment is life; it is liberated life, and to be the prey of maladjustment is to approach pain and misery. Everything within the environment is all right; the only difficulty is found in the conception of selfish special interest. Our aversion to the universal interest is the cause of our detachment from the conception of the whole and from happiness and health. We have been deprived of the happiness of our healthy position, and the cause is selfish interest.

The Absolute Autocrat is absolute good. So there is no room for complaint against Him. Krishna says: *suhṛdaṁ sarva-bhūtānām*. He is the owner of everything; in comparison, we are nothing. But still, He is our friend. We should not forget that. We are represented in Him. Our detachment from Him is the cause of all the miseries that we are suffering. We and others like us have lost faith in Him, but

He is our friend. We are jealous of Him and are thinking, "I am not the master? Someone else is the master – this is intolerable. No taxation without representation!" But our interests are well-represented in Krishna. He cares about us even more than we can conceive. Why do we forget that?

If we only reinstate ourselves in that faith, we will be all right. It is our fault that we are suffering; otherwise there is no difference in vision from the universal standpoint. *Īśād apetasya*, we have turned away from our master. But we should remember that He is our master, He is our well-wisher, He is our guardian. Deviation from that consciousness is misery of an infinite magnitude. Its cause is very subtle and very minute; it is our mentality of separate interest. And as a result, we have been captured by the enemy camp.

Patañjali has said we are moving towards evil in an intelligent, organized way. That is not only mad but wicked; it is worse than mad, according to Patañjali. What will be the relief of a soul in such a deplorable condition? A madman is in possession of everything – he is only out of his mind. His consciousness has to be adjusted properly. Then he will find, "Oh, everything is all right – let me go back home." At present his consciousness is cast aside. He is not at home; his consciousness must be pushed homeward.

That is the problem. Our Guru Mahārāj used to say, "I don't admit any famine in this world – only that of a lack of Krishna consciousness: *jagate eka mātra hari-kathā-durvikṣā chāḍ'a āra kona durvikṣā nāi.*" Whenever he became excited, he used to use this expression. He would say:

"From door to door tell everyone, 'Krishna is the Supreme, you are all servants of Krishna.' Remind everyone of this, from door to door. Then they will find, 'Oh, I have everything I need. I am Krishna-*dāsa*, a servant of Krishna. I must connect with Krishna.' That link must be supplied, and then everything will be all right. There is no dearth of anything else. There is no real misery, except that we have forgotten Krishna, our Lord. That is the only point we must push. This is the universal necessity. I don't admit any necessity besides this."

Within this world there is always a fire burning; but there is no necessity of extinguishing the fire, because we have nothing to do with the world that will be burned into ashes by the fire. All our inner demands can be met only in connection with Krishna. All other things are unnecessary. They may be burned into ashes or devoured by flood. We have no real concern with any of those things. Rather, those material attachments are dragging us back towards the wrong thing. And as a result, we can't allow our mind to be attracted to Krishna. The things of this world, or attachments, are all negative; these things are all our enemy. The whole universe may be burned to ashes, but we will not be affected in any way. The world may be devastated – the Earth, the sun, the moon, the stars – everything may vanish, but still we remain. The soul is eternal. And if we can have a connection with Krishna, the things of this world are all unnecessary for us and for everyone else. Why should we come to live in the mortal world, erroneously identifying ourselves with flesh and blood? We only think that we are being born and dying. But it is a false notion.

Everything is conscious. And when we realize it fully, we shall be fixed in the *svarūpa-śakti* domain in the spiritual world. There, the different living beings may pose as matter, as the Yamunā, as water, as creepers, as trees, but they are all conscious units, simply posing in different ways.

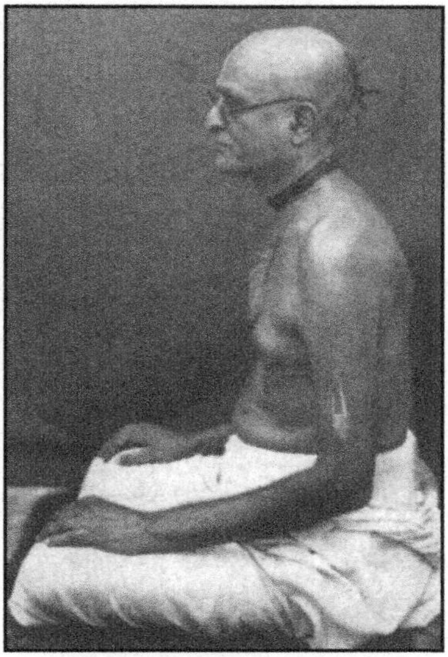

Śrīla Bhaktisiddhānta Saraswatī Ṭhākura

Dr. Murphey: It is said that when Krishna goes to take bath in the Yamunā, all the waves rush in to embrace Krishna.

Śrīla Śrīdhar Mahārāj: Sometimes the stones melt feeling the imprint of Krishna's lotus feet. Everything is conscious. So it is also in the case of Rāhu and Ketu and other planets. Everywhere in the scriptures, the spiritually developed sages are found talking with nature as if they are talking with a person. And it is real. But our consciousness is deviated in ignorance.

So as scientists, you must crush the philosophy of fossilism. Bhaktivedānta Swāmī Mahārāja has ordered you to take a strong position in the scientific community in the West and crush fossilism. Why should we accept fossilism?

First there is consciousness. This is Berkeley's theory. Not that mind is in the world, but world is in the mind. Everything is based on consciousness; no conception – nothing remains – without consciousness. So ultimately all undesirable things are only a mental concoction.

The Creation

Śrīla Śrīdhar Mahārāj: The *Mānu Saṁhitā (1.1.5-6)* begins describing the creation from this point:

āsīd idaṁ tamo bhūtam
aprajñātam alakṣanam
apratarkyam avijñeyaṁ
prasuptam iva sarvataḥ

tataḥ svayambhur bhāgavān
avyaktavyaṁ jayan idam
mahābhutādi vṛtaujāḥ
prādur āsin tamonudaḥ

Just before the creative movement began, the marginal potency of the Lord was in a state of equilibrium. *Taṭasthā* means equilibrium: *āsīd idaṁ tamo bhūtam*. Everything was in darkness, fully enveloped by ignorance. *Alakṣanam* means there was no possibility of any estimation; no symptoms of reality existed by which any conjecture or inference about the nature of reality would have been possible. And it was *aprajñatam*: science has no capacity for investigating the nature of that stage of existence. We can only say from here that it was completely immersed in deep sleep. The analogy of deep sleep may give us some conception of that period: *prasuptam iva sarvataḥ*. Material existence was as if in a sound sleep.

At that time, movement began from within the spiritual plane, and light came. Light was seen by the seers. That light was pre-existent, but at that time the seers received the vision to see light. They began to see. The first conception of this material world after light was water. The light revealed a substance like water.

That primal light is compared with personality. Light means consciousness and consciousness means personality. That light, or personality, first gave birth to the onlookers – to the feelers of material existence – and then to an objective substance like water. That water is known as *virajā*, or causal substance. What is known in Vaiṣṇava vocabulary as *brahmaloka* – the world of consciousness – is represented by light, and *virajā*, or causal substance, is represented by water. The conscious world is represented by light and the first objective reality is represented as water. Then the seeds of consciousness are sown in the causal water which is the shadow of that light. Although the actual element of water was created long after this, the first conception of matter is compared to water because water is an accommodating, moving solution. The Sanskrit word for water, *apa*, means "of lower conception." In this way, the lower creation began.

Then, in connection with the seeds of consciousness and the primal water, the next production was known as *mahat-tattva*: the energy of consciousness represented by light, mixed with matter as a mass. When the mass of matter is infused with the energy of light-consciousness, that is known as *mahat-tattva*.

After further development, that entity was divided into many units of *ahaṅkara*, the element of ego. *Mahato ahaṅkara*. First there is *ahaṅkara*, mass ego as a whole. The element of conglomerate ego is called *mahat-tattva*. As objective substance evolves by the influence of consciousness, it expresses itself in five main ingredients: that which can be seen, smelled, heard, tasted, and touched. These five elements are the primitive principles of material existence.

And that fivefold principle evolved in three phases: *sattva, raja, tamah*: goodness, passion, and ignorance. Expressing itself as ether, sound, hearing, and the ear; air, mass, touch, and the skin; fire, color, vision, and the eye; water, tastes, the sense of taste, and the tongue; and earth, aroma, the sense of smell, and the nose. There are twenty-four elements. The self, three subtle elements – *prakṛti, mahat-tattva*, and *ahaṅkara*, five gross elements, five senses, five sense objects, five sense-gathering instruments – in this way, the development of the material world has been described to have come down through a process of subtle to gross, from consciousness to matter. Again when this material existence is withdrawn by superior will, the gross dissolves into the subtle. Beginning with the most gross, gradually the whole of material existence becomes more and more subtle until it finally enters into the subtle expression of material existence known as *prakṛti* – the subtle causal watery substance.

With the dissolution of material energy, the *ātmā* or individual soul is absorbed in *brahman*, the nondifferentiated mass of consciousness. The position of the different kinds of spiritual energy has been described by Krishna in *Bhagavad-gītā (15.16)* as follows:

dvāv imau puruṣau loke
kṣaraś cākṣara eva ca
kṣaraḥ sarvāṇi bhūtāni
kūṭa-stho 'kṣara ucyate

uttamaḥ puruṣas tv anyaḥ
paramātmety udāhṛtaḥ
yo loka-trayam āviśya
bibharty avyaya īśvaraḥ

"There are two kinds of beings – the perfect and unchanging, or infallible, and the fallible souls. The fallible souls reside in the material world and the infallible souls reside in the spiritual world." Krishna says, "I exist, transcending both fallible and infallible aspects of spiritual substance *(kṣara and akṣara)*, so I am Puruṣottama, Vāsudeva, Param Brahma, the Supreme Absolute Truth. Within Me the whole of my jurisdiction is also to be considered."

Vaikuṇṭha, Goloka – the whole creation – is represented by the name of Puruṣottama or Vāsudeva. Then, when one enters into that domain of Vāsudeva, he can see so many demarcations, stages of reality, pastimes, and transcendental dealings and activities. There he will find the perfected living beings busy in their dedicated life in the eternal world.

The general conception of the spiritual world is Vaikuṇṭha wherein we find calculative dedication. Above that is the plane of spontaneous dedication. That realm is called Goloka, and there are many different kinds of pastimes there. In Goloka, all the various relationships with Godhead are represented in full: *śānta*, passive, *dāsya*, servitude, *sakhya*, friendship, *vātsalya*, parenthood, *mādhura*, conjugal. And the conjugal mellow can be subdivided into *svakīya*, wedded love, and *parakīya*, a paramour relationship. This is, of course, a very elevated subject matter. Still, we have to have some view of these things since our fate is ultimately connected with such high things, given to us by Śrī Caitanya Mahāprabhu and great *āchāryas* like Bhaktivinoda Ṭhākura and discussed in scriptures like *Śrīmad-Bhāgavatam* and *Chaitanya-caritāmṛta*.

What is found in their teachings about Goloka is our prospect, our aspiration. According to our devotional taste we will develop, and our taste can also be improved by hearing from a higher source. The spirit of our selection may be improved when we are shown different ideas, different models of transcendental reality. And according to what attracts us most based upon our inner choice, we shall have to act.

Question: What part do the individual souls play in the process of creation?

Śrīla Śrīdhar Mahārāj: I have described that. At first a general, conglomerate false ego (*ahaṅkara*) is created. This is called *śambhu* in *Brahma-Saṁhitā*, wherein it explains how the soul as a ray of consciousness mingles with material energy. Consciousness and *prakṛti*, the most primitive conceptions of energy, are categorically different. The conglomerate consciousness comes in contact with mass energy, and as they mingle together, a general ego evolves. That general ego gradually dissolves into innumerable egos, and the conglomerate consciousness distributes itself as individual units of consciousness absorbed in material energy. In this way, gradually, the individual conditioned souls come down and are entangled within the material world.

In a primitive state when the individual souls are massed together as a common whole, the conglomerate false-ego, or *ahaṅkara*, is known as *mahat-tattva*. As it evolves, it differentiates into innumerable individual units. Just as an atom can be broken down into subatomic particles, electrons, protons, neutrons and so on, the conglomerate ego gradually breaks into its component individual egos, *jīva* souls. Their position is *taṭastha*, marginal, and undetectable. From that subtle, undetectable plane of marginal energy, consciousness first develops into the detectable plane as a whole, and then innumerable individual spiritual units are manifest from that mass lump of ego, or *mahat-tattva*. Gradually, the other elements of creation develop within this negative plane of exploitation.

This world is sometimes pushing forth, and sometimes withdrawing. In the same way that the heart expands and contracts again and again, the whole universe expands and contracts. Regrouping within the one, and again manifest as the many – the one and the many – the evolution and dissolution of the material universe takes place. As a heart expands and contracts, the whole universe is manifest and withdrawn.

The same characteristics that we find in the smallest unit can be traced in the bigger units. This is the suggestion by which we may know the whole, more or less. There are also some categorically new elements to be added to our knowledge. In this way, those who are within this universe can have some partial knowledge.

But those who are independent, outside the contracting and expanding world, who are impartial onlookers, can give the real history. That is the revealed truth, which is distributed in installments according to the capacity of the people, of the time, place and circumstance. The revealed truth is found in varying degrees in the Bible, the Koran, the *Vedas*, and the other scriptures of the world. Through this process, the truth is partially revealed in different places of the world in proportion to the thinking and capacity of each particular group of people. The revealed truth is reliable, but still it is modified to fit the persons to whom it is extended.

For that reason we find differences in the different versions of the revealed truth. It is said in *Śrīmad-Bhāgavatam* that medicine may be hidden within candy to treat the ignorant; in the same way, the revealed truth may be hidden within the mundane concessions of ordinary religion to help the ignorant class of men, *parokṣavāda vedo 'yam*.

Still, Vedic revelation is conceived of by authorities as the most ancient as well as the most perfect of all versions of revealed truth. The revealed truth as presented by *Śrīmad-Bhāgavatam* and Śrī Caitanya Mahāprabhu must be considered full-fledged theism. There it is mentioned what lies beyond this created world is the eternally dancing world. Here we are trapped in the world of contraction and expansion, but in the spiritual realm, everything is an eternal, blissful dance. Still, even the reality there is of a lower and higher type according to the nature of *rasa* – transcendental mellow, *ānandam*, ecstasy – which is the desired substance of every conscious unit.

Question: Krishna's pastimes are eternal. When Krishna finishes one pastime in this universe, his pastimes begin in another. At the time of the final annihilation, when all the universes are withdrawn, how do Krishna's pastimes continue?

Śrīla Śrīdhar Mahārāj: When the universe is destroyed in the total annihilation of all the stars and planets, the *mahāpralaya*, this side almost equates to zero. It reaches equilibrium. But the spiritual world is always in full swing. No harm can be done to Krishna's pastimes because they have an eternal aspect.

Question: But what happens to Krishna's *līlā* here on Earth?

Śrīla Śrīdhar Mahārāj: Suppose fruit falls from a tree. The fruit is gradually finished, but the tree remains. It is something like that. This material world may equate to zero, but Krishna's pastimes continue eternally.

Question: What is the difference between Goloka, Krishna's place of pastimes in the transcendent world, and Gokula, Krishna's pleasure abode in this earthly plane?

Śrīla Śrīdhar Mahārāj: Gokula Vṛndāvana eternally exists, but sometimes the seers are all absent. Gokula exists in the ideal world and is extended here. What we see, we see from our different positions of existence, but Gokula is there always. If you have no eye to see something, it cannot be seen. If you have no hand to touch it, it cannot be touched. It is the same with Gokula. It is in such a plane where the different external processes which exert control over material energy cannot touch the fine ideal of existence in Gokula.

If the earth vanishes, that does not mean that the whole solar system will vanish. The solar system may remain, but the men on the earth cannot see it any longer. Its influence on earth can no longer be felt. In a similar way, Gokula exists in another plane. It exists in the finest plane of reality. It is beyond the creation, beyond evolution and dissolution. Such subtle energy can be understood by analogy with ether. If earth is destroyed, ether may not be destroyed. Ether is within and outside earth, but with the dissolution of earth, ether may not dissolve, but continue to exist. The position of Gokula is something like that. This is confirmed by *Śrīmad-Bhāgavatam (2.9.35):*

yathā mahānti bhūtāni
bhūteṣūccāvaceṣv anu

praviṣṭāny apraviṣṭāni
tathā teṣu na teṣv aham

"O Brahmā, please know that the universal elements enter into the cosmos and at the same time do not enter into the cosmos; similarly, I also exist within everything and at the same time I am outside everything."

Krishna's position is similar: He is there and not there. In *Bhagavad-gītā (9.4-5),* He tells Arjuna:

mayā tatam idaṁ sarvaṁ
jagad avyakta-mūrtinā
mat-sthāni sarva-bhūtāni
na cāhaṁ teṣv avasthitaḥ

na ca mat-sthāni bhūtāni
paśya me yogam aiśvaram
bhūta-bhṛn na ca bhūta-stho
mamātmā bhūta-bhāvanaḥ

"I am everywhere and nowhere. Everything is in Me, and yet nothing is in Me. In My unmanifested form, this entire universe is pervaded. Behold My mystic opulence, My simultaneous oneness and difference! Although I am the maintainer of all living entities and although I am everywhere, I am not implicated by any of this, for I am the very source of creation."

We have to understand the relationship between cause and effect. The cause and its effect are of different types. Even the inner cause and the outer cause may have different positions. The body may be disturbed, but the mind may not be. The mind may be disturbed, the soul may not be. By this we are to understand the difference between cause and effect, subtle and gross, matter and spirit.

Consciousness & Evolution

Prakṛti, the material nature, does not evolve consciousness like fossilism. But on the other hand, both are within consciousness. There is no necessity of movement for the soul here. The soul is inactive, indifferent, passive in this enjoying plane. That is another original conception. The soul does not take its place in the negative side; it is meant for the positive side. But accepting that the soul is in the background, *prakṛti* or material energy – the body – works on its behalf. The relationship between body and soul is like the relationship between a minor and his false guardians. It is something like what happens when the proprietor of an estate is a minor and the managers take advantage of his youth to loot and enjoy the estate. The *baddha-jīva* soul is in the minor's position. The soul cannot control these revolting managers, the five senses. He need only have the contact of a major soul. With the help and guidance of the major soul, he can subdue his managers and gain mastery over his own property. A fallen soul's position is like a minor proprietor. He is helpless. He is doing nothing: the managers are doing everything using his own resources;

they are doing everything in the name of the proprietor. The soul is inactive, non-cooperating. But the body, mind, intelligence, and false-ego are working on behalf of the soul – the real ego – as if he were on their side. But if his real interest inside is roused by a major soul who is connected with Paramātmā and with Bhagavān, then the soul will find his own field there. He'll control the senses and mind and utilize them in the service of the Lord. He'll say, "Everything is for Krishna, not for me."

So Krishna says, *sarva-dharmān parityajya mām ekaṁ śaraṇaṁ vraja*: "Give up all your duties and come to Me. And your present duties good or bad, whatever you can conceive from your present position – give up everything and come straight to Me. I'm everything to you." This is Krishna consciousness. Krishna is telling us: "You belong to me, you are My property. Just as you can say that you are master of any property, so you are My property, My slave." That is the truth, and by accepting that truth we will live in a higher plane. We will be the gainer, we will come into our normal position. At present, in an abnormal position, we are suffering from thinking, "I'm the master, the monarch of all I survey." But that ego is our worst enemy if we are to progress in devotional service.

And service to Krishna is of different varieties. There is service in general and then there are services of a particular type: *śānta*, *dāsya*, *sakhya*, *vātsalya*, *mādhura*. And then there are also divisions according to whether devotion is calculative or spontaneous. In this way there is a hierarchy in the development of the devotional condition.

The highest development is *ujjvala-rasa. Ujjvala-rasa* means super-fine, the brightest, surpassing all, where we find Krishna in consorthood without any consideration of any law. Autocratic consorthood. And this particular nature and behavior is described in a book written by Rūpa Goswāmī titled *Ujjvala-nīlamaṇi*. The first part of devotion is given in *Bhakti-rasāmṛta-sindhu*. In that book, from the very beginning of an ordinary civilized religious life, Rūpa Goswāmī takes us up to different devotional relationships *śānta*, *dāsya*, *sakhya*, *vātsalya*, and *mādhura-rasa*. But the details of *mādhura-rasa*, the highest relationship with Krishna, has been described by Rūpa Goswāmī in *Ujjvala-nīlamaṇi*. Nīlamaṇi, Krishna, in his highest luster: *ujjvala*. Nīlamaṇi in consorthood. And what are Krishna's characteristics? How does he play with his paraphernalia in the *mādhura-rasa*? That has been described in detail in *Ujjvala-nīlamaṇi*.

Even the greatest literary scholars are dumbfounded to find how divine love has been analyzed so finely and elaborately in this book of Rūpa Goswāmī. Subtle points have been analyzed, organized, and distributed in that book. And the great scholars become dumbfounded when they come to such statements. As *Bhāgavatam* says: *muhyanti yat sūrayaḥ*. In the introduction, *Bhāgavatam* gives this warning, this caution to the scholars: "You will all be dumbfounded when you attempt to come to this plane. Scholarship will not allow you to flourish here." The nature of that plane is so mysterious that even great scholars won't be considered fit to enter there.

Only the surrendered souls can understand and feel these subtle points of devotion. Outsiders, who remain objective inquirers and researchers, can't have any entrance here. It is the superior subjective realm, the supersubjective realm. That plane is above even the plane of soul.

And to understand this, we must first inquire about the soul. First there is mind, *manaḥ*, then intelligence, *buddhi*, then soul, *ātmā*. The soul is evergreen: it does not die. Soul is eternal, constant. It is said in the *Upaniṣads* and in the *Gītā:* if once we can meet our soul, then a diametrical change comes in our life. At that time we will be astonished to realize, "Oh, such a highly qualified thing is here within me! In ignorance, I was considering that this perishable body and this flickering mind, was my true self. But the material senses and mind are all trespassers, they have some inimical tendency towards my true self. I am soul: I have no necessity of all these things. Without these unnecessary material things I can live! No food is necessary for the soul from the jurisdiction of this material plane. The soul is independent. What a wonderful existence I have! In reality I am soul, and the nature of soul is so noble, so high, so good." A diametrical change of consciousness comes at this point and one tries to enter into that higher realm. Spiritual reality is what is necessary for us. We are soul, we are independent of matter. We are made of such transcendental existence. Nothing can threaten the soul's existence – not the atomic bomb, nuclear war, lightning, thunder, or earthquakes. All the troubles of this material world are limited to this body which is a foreign carcass, a concocted representation of my true self. My true self exists on the spiritual plane, on a higher level. If we can really have a touch of that realization, a glimpse of our own identity – if we can feel within that the soul is independent of matter, then a revolutionary change will take place within our minds. Then our attempt to progress in spiritual life becomes quite genuine. Otherwise, our progress is suspicious, doubtful. We grasp it intellectually, and think, "Yes, let me try. I'm hearing, of course, that I have a good prospect in spiritual life; by my intelligence I can follow something. Let me try." But progress on the intellectual plane is only hesitating progress. When one comes to the plane of one's own soul, however, one will find one's self and realize, "Here I am!" At that time all false conceptions which have been held for so long will vanish like a dream. They will all be finished, and one will think, "I'm to start a new life." And the new prospect will open to make progress in the higher plane.

Soul is nearby. We can try to find out what the soul is if we can eliminate the material elements. This is the process of the *Upaniṣads* and is mentioned in the *Bhagavad-gītā: indriyāṇi parāṇy āhur (3.42).* First we are to understand that our senses are primary. If my senses are removed, the entire world of our experience is nothing to me. Only through my senses can I be aware of the existence of the outside world. Minus senses, eyes, ears, no world is apparent to me. Then, above the senses is the mind. What is the mind? The mind deals with acceptance and rejection: *saṅkalpa vikalpa.* In other words, the mind thinks, "I want this, I don't want that." It deals with attachment and hatred. The mind determines who is enemy and who is friend, this is mine, that's yours. If we want to understand the mind we have to look within, to inquire within: what is that element in me that seeks friends and avoids enemies? Where is he? Sometimes the mind is apparent; then other times it is hiding. I must find out where the mind exists, of what substance is it composed? By analysis I can understand what aspect of my inner self is the mind. Then, having some idea of what the mind is, I may analyze that part of me which deals with reason, the intelligence. Where is the intelligence?

When the mind demands something; the intelligence says, "Don't take that, don't eat that." By introspection, I may look within and find out: what is that principle in me which reasons? Where is that fine thing? What is its nature, its substance, its existence? We shall try in our introspection to find it out, substantially. If that is possible, then the next step will take us to the soul. What is that soul which makes possible the intelligence, the reason by which we act, which prompts the mind to want, and also gives our senses the power to connect with things? What is that spark of knowledge? Where is that soul within me? What position does it hold ? I want to see it face to face. Then in this way we can evaporate like lightning all the misconceptions of body and mind. By finding the soul through introspection, we may experience the lightning touch of realization.

At that time, the whole world will be turned in a diametrically different line, and we shall see things differently:

In Milton's Paradise Lost, Satan said, "It is better to reign in hell than serve in heaven." But we shall experience just the opposite: "It is better to serve in heaven than to reign in hell."

"Oh, this material life is undesirable! These senses are enemies in the garb of friends. If I confront them now, they say that I may have an honorable friendship with them, and that without them I can't live. But it is all a hoax."

From a realization of the soul, from the point of that wonderful knowledge, one may come to see the ocean of knowledge. One may begin to see what is in the subjective area, and hanker for how to come in connection with that divine realm. At that time, the very trend of one's life will be changed, and a total change will come in our search, in our standard of prospect in life. And our search will take a concrete shape in devotion. In this way, we must begin our search after the higher sphere. And how to enter there?

It is the opposite of this plane of exploitation. In Milton's *Paradise Lost*, Satan said, "It is better to reign in hell than serve in heaven." But we shall experience just the opposite: "It is better to serve in heaven than to reign in hell." To serve in heaven is highly superior than to reign in hell.

The question of energy and power is important in the mortal world, but in the constant and eternal world, this sort of energy has no value. That plane is composed of eternal substance. It is not like this troubling plane which is always breaking, always disappearing, always disappointing, and full of treachery. That divine plane is constant. Life goes on there without any need of food, rest, or medicine. There is no need of the labor to earn bread in that higher realm. All these things are not necessary in a plane of reality where everything is permanent and of eternal value. All these problems which are making us madly busy are easily eliminated in one stroke. That is the nature of that plane. And if we realize that we are members of that plane, then the question becomes what to do? How to approach the higher realm? That will be our problem. We cannot force our entry there; we must be granted a visa. We cannot master that finer realm – we must allow ourselves to be utilized by it. In other words we must come to the position of slavery. We shall have to realize that mastership here in the mortal world is a curse, and the slavery in that higher world is a boon.

And the *Bhāgavatam* will help us in our progressive march towards that higher plane.

naṣṭa-prāyeṣv abhadreṣu
nityaṁ bhāgavata-sevayā
bhagavaty uttama-śloke
bhaktir bhavati naiṣṭhikī

The impure, undesirable things within us are going to

almost completely vanish, almost disappear by our serving association with the *Śrīmad-Bhāgavatam* and the devotee. *Sādhu* and *śāstra*. In this way, the continuous connection with Krishna consciousness comes out from within. The interrupting elements that result from renunciation and enjoyment vanish, the covers vanish, and the continuous flow within, the connection with pure Krishna consciousness comes out.

There are two covers: the exploiting tendency and the renouncing tendency – *karma* and *jñāna* – the exploiting spirit and the tendency for knowledge that leads to liberation. They are not proper elements of our soul, of our real entity; they are only covers. And by our serving association with the *Śrīmad-Bhāgavatam* and the devotee, they are uncovered, and the continuous flow of Krishna consciousness within comes out.

Niṣṭhā means *nairantaja*, continuous.

ādau śraddhā tataḥ sādhu-
saṅgo'tha bhajana-kriyā
tato'nartha-nivṛttiḥ syāt
tato niṣṭhā rucis tataḥ

When the covers are removed, then we find that inner continuity of flow with Krishna connection within us, and *naiṣthikī-bhakti* appears That is completely clear, cleansed. *Bhaktir bhavati naiṣthikī:* then on the basis of *niṣṭhā*, that is, the continuous flow, then further progress is made on the positive side – *āsakti*, attachment, then *bhāva*, spiritual emotion, then *prema*, divine love – in this way the inner

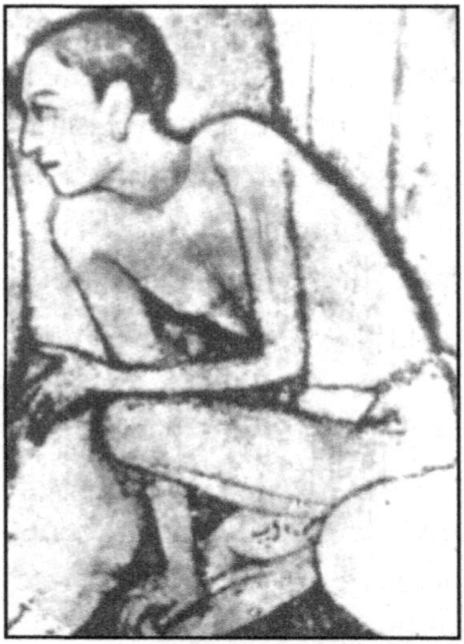
Śrīla Rupa Goswāmī

aspect of devotion will gradually come out. And we shall be able to dive deep into reality. As we give up the external covers, and we experience what may be considered as death in the external world – die to live – we shall enter into the inner side more and more.

Question: This verse says *naṣṭa-prāyeṣv abhadreṣu*, that the impurities are almost destroyed. Why not completely destroyed?

Śrīla Śrīdhar Mahārāj: That means it happens gradually. The gradual development is described there. *Naṣṭa prāyeṣu* means when the stage of *niṣṭhā* comes, when all the undesirabilities are almost finished, then we can have a real peep into the thing. Just as before sunrise, when there is twilight in the early morning, the sun is not there, but the darkness has been dispelled. The darkness has been mainly removed, but the sun has not yet risen. In the same way, the *Bhāgavatam* is describing how *bhakti* develops gradually. *Naṣṭa prāyeṣu*: it is not finished immediately; there is a gradual process of *sādhana* – a means to an end. And gradually, slowly, according to the capacity of the devotee, and the endeavor, the *sādhana*, one's *bhakti* develops. When darkness has almost been finished, the non-gentle, abnormal, exploitative symptoms like the mean attempt to exploit the environment, gradually disappear. And in this way, gradually, we make further progress. It is not that all of a sudden – in one stroke – everything is cleared. Rather, according to our *bhajana*, our *sādhana*, our attempt, the undesirable elements will gradually vanish, go away. And by different stages we shall reach the goal.

These stages have been described by Rūpa Goswāmī as follows in his *Bhakti-rasāmṛta-sindhu (1.4.15-16):*

ādau śraddhā tataḥ sādhu-
saṅgo'tha bhajana-kriyā
tato'nartha-nivṛttiḥ syāt
tato niṣṭhā rucis tataḥ
athāsaktis tato bhāvas
tataḥ premābhyudañcati
sādhakānām ayaṁ premṇaḥ
prādurbhāve bhavet kramaḥ

"In the beginning there must be faith. Then one becomes interested in associating with pure devotees. Thereafter one is initiated by the spiritual master and executes the regulative principles under his orders. Thus one is freed from all unwanted habits and becomes firmly fixed in devotional service. Thereafter, one develops taste and then attachment. This is the way of *sādhana-bhakti*, the execution of devotional service according to the regulative principles. Gradually spiritual emotions manifest and intensify, then finally there is an awakening of divine love. This is the gradual development of love of Godhead for the devotee interested in Krishna consciousness."

Rūpa Goswāmī says that *niṣṭhā* means "continuous connection." After *niṣṭhā*, the mundane negative side is eliminated, and then, in the positive side, we may make progress. Then, after this there are the higher stages: *āsakti, bhāva,* and *prema*. Within *prema*, there are also different stages: *sneha, mana, rāga, anurāga, bhāva, mahābhāva.* In this way *bhakti* develops to the topmost plane, *mahābhāva. Mahābhāva* means Rādhārāṇī. That supermost intensity of *bhakti* which is not found anywhere else is found only in Her. That is called *mahābhāva*. In this way, *bhakti* – divine love – develops in different stages up to the highest level.

The Plane of Misconception

This chapter is an excerpt from a conversation between Śrīla Śrīdhar Mahārāj and neurophysiologist Dr. Daniel Murphey, physical organic chemist Dr. Thoudam Singh, and Dr. Michael Marchetti.

We should understand that we are living in the plane of misconception. The whole thing is false. It is all a part of illusion. Within the world of illusion, some thing may have its place, but when we deal with the real truth, however, we will conclude that everything here is like a dream. This whole world is like a dream, a misconception. Any part of this world will therefore also be misconception. What is real, what is truth, will become apparent when a thing is judged in connection with the real world. The association of saints who have a genuine connection with spiritual reality promotes this transaction.

What is real and what is unreal? Whatever has a connection with the real self, with the soul, is real. Soul is consciousness in the world of pure consciousness. Whatever is connected with the mind in the mental world of false-ego is all false. A part of the false is also false, extremely false. But it has got its negative utility.

Everything is true only by having connection with the Absolute Truth. Everything is there in the absolute. So the finite cannot produce anything which is not in the infinite. The finite world, therefore, is rather a shadow or a perverted reflection of the whole truth.

The foundation of my argument is as follows: Caitanya Mahāprabhu explained that while Śaṅkarāchārya has denied the existence of this perverted reflection, we cannot dismiss it. If it does not exist, then why has Śaṅkara come to preach Vedanta? Illusion means "this is not that." One thing may appear to be some thing else. An illusion is not what it appears to be, but it is not nonexistent. In that way it is real. It has its existence.

Within the real world which is created by the help of the Lord's internal energy, *svarūpa-śakti*, this world of misconception has no place. But in a relative way, the conditioned world has an indirect relationship with the unconditioned world. So *māyā* is existing. In that sense it is true. But it is false in that it cannot give you the desired result you are searching after. In that sense it is all false.

Dr. Marchetti: Vaiṣṇavism says that this material nature is real as a reflection. But it is not real as the absolute reality of the spiritual world. Could you explain?

Śrīla Śrīdhar Mahārāj: Reality is composed of unreal substance and real substance. We may see it like that. This is the world of misconception. Misconception means "I think something is mine, but really it is not mine." Everything belongs to the Absolute. Everything belongs to him. But we say "it is mine," and we quarrel with each other. Actually, everything within this world is the property of another. But as a result of misconception, we fight with each other and so many reactions result from that fight. The difficulty is that the soul is entangled in this mock fight. Otherwise this world of fighting and misconception has no value. But the dust of spirit, a very infinitesimal part of the spiritual reality, is entangled in this world and concerned with this world of mock fighting. Without the spiritual energy within this world, nothing would remain. A magician's sleight of hand is all based on misconception. It is false. Still we are perplexed by his tactics. That is also true. A magician or hypnotist can show what is not real to be real, and yet while we are under his spell we cannot deny its reality.

Everything, including our own self, belongs to Krishna. But the difficulty arises when we see something other than Krishna. Separate interest. The consciousness of separate interest is the root of all evils. We are one with Krishna, but whenever the seed of separate interest sprouts, and we think we have some separate interest, that we are not included in the interest of Krishna, that is the root of such misconception.

bhayaṁ dvitīyābhiniveśatah syād
īśād apetasya viparyayo 'smṛtiḥ
tan-māyayāto budha ābhajet taṁ
bhaktyaikayeśaṁ guru-devatātmā

In this way, the scriptures have given a diagnosis of the disease or concoction of false conception. We are living in a fool's paradise. And the very beginning of material existence that we can trace is at the inception of a separate interest. The first deviation from *advaya-jñāna* is a conception of separate interest.

Question: How can we know what is actually real?

Śrīla Śrīdhar Mahārāj: The scriptural name is *śraddhā*, or faith. That is the developed state of *sukṛti,* or spiritual merit. When our faith is developed, it leads us to *sādhu saṅga*, the association of saints. The agents of the divine world, who are in the plane of reality – the *nirguṇa* wave beyond this world of creation – come to establish some connection with reality in our soul. That is the deepest element. The connection with saints produces faith, and faith can see reality.

There is a world which is only approachable by faith *śraddhāmayo'yaṁ loka*. Just as color is seen by the eyes and sound is perceived by the ear, that world can be perceived only by faith. Only faith can see and feel it. The Supreme Reality cannot be perceived with any other senses. Faith is the real function of the soul and that is awakened by the agents of Vaikuṇṭha, the saints. By faith one's association with saints increases, and by this transaction the culture of reality takes place. Gradually this process makes us become fully conscious. At that time we realize that this world in which we are living is all transient and that our home is elsewhere. Our real home is located in the world of pure consciousness.

Śrīla Bhaktivedānta Swāmī Mahārāj

Question: Is that the same process by which the materialist sees this world as real?

Śrīla Śrīdhar Mahārāj: No. Realization of spiritual reality is independent of all material contamination or misconception. That injection into our soul is given by Vaikuṇṭha, by the eternal associates of Viṣṇu. Perceiving spiritual reality is the function of the soul, not of the material ego or senses. It is independent of that. When a patient is unconscious, the doctor gives him an injection. Then consciousness comes and after that he can cooperate with the doctor by describing his symptoms. But before one can cooperate with the doctor, the doctor does different things to help the unconscious patient. In the same way, when we are fully engrossed in our material engagement, the saints from the higher plane of reality act like doctors to inject some understanding of divinity into our consciousness. In this way they try to awaken our spiritual self-interest, our consciousness of the soul.

Dr. Singh: Once Bhaktivedānta Swāmī Mahārāj asked us to prove that matter comes from life, by using science. I didn't know how to start. How can we prove that matter comes from life?

Śrīla Śrīdhar Mahārāj: The definition of evolution given by Darwin is that life comes from the fossil. But we say just the opposite. Evolution from inside of consciousness is the cause of our seeing the different things of this world. The evolution is from within. Evolution is not from the outside, as we might ordinarily think. This is the teaching of Vedānta. Reality does not develop from imperfection to perfection; it is only that a part of the perfection seems to be imperfect. To theorize that the imperfect is producing perfection is ludicrous.

It is far more reasonable and easy to conceive that a part of the perfection has somehow become imperfect. It is perceived by us to be imperfect. That is the natural and more reasonable conclusion. We have to accept something of what Darwin says but where does the fossil come from? And that the fossil can produce the infinite is a foolish idea.

The body is amazing the doctors with so many wonderful phenomena. They cannot fathom so many questions. How is it built? How are consciousness, intelligence, and genius centered in the brain? That wonderful thing which we find in the brain, the thought of the genius, is not produced by a material thing. The starting point must be the wonderful thing. We say that really exists – that wonderful thing, the source of all wonders.

Everything is full of wonder. If we analyze the atom, we will be in wonder. Only we impose limitations. But when we analyze the atomic parts of wood or stone, we will be in wonder. The infinite is everywhere. Perfection is everywhere. The trouble is that with our limited thinking we have produced a world of limits. But we who are captured by the "scientific" way of thinking are not ready to admit that. That is the puzzle. From the biggest to the smallest, from the lowest to the highest, everything is wonderful. But we won't admit that. We will go to the fossil and say that the fossil is producing everything. But what is that fossil?

Dr. Marchetti: But how can we prove to the scientists that matter comes from life? These are philosophical arguments. The scientists will say, "What is the utility of philosophical arguments?"

Śrīla Śrīdhar Mahārāj: In the beginning of the electric generation, the famous scientist Michael Faraday gave a public demonstration of the power of electricity. In one experiment, Faraday generated electricity. With the current generated by his dynamo, he was able to move some pieces of paper. After watching the wave of current move some pieces of paper, a lady challenged him, "What is the utility of your electricity, Dr. Faraday?" And he said, "Madam, would you please tell me, what is the utility of a newborn babe?"

Is death philosophical? Death is there to frustrate all other things if you don't take shelter in philosophy. Only philosophy can face the greatest enemy, death. And death is not limited to a particular thing; it will include the whole world. The sun, the moon, the stars, this globe, and everything else will vanish in due course of time. The scientists themselves tell us so. If we want to live beyond the plane of death, philosophy will help us have an eternal life of eternal

Charles Darwin

peace. Only philosophy can give us that.

All these sciences of technology are simply an attempt to increase the glamour of this life. They are all enemies of the soul, deadly enemies. All of them lead us but to the grave. The grave is true and only dealing with the grave philosophically will relieve us. Otherwise, we are all finished. These materialistic scientific conceptions are cunning enemies surrounding us. They are tempting us, "Live in the material world. We shall help you." This is illusion.

Dr. Marchetti: When you said that the world is in the mind, isn't that idealism?

Śrīla Śrīdhar Mahārāj: Berkeley's idealism: not that we are in the world, but the world is in our mind. Of course in a higher sense, we are not concerned with the mind. The material mind is also a part of the world of misconception. The soul is living in the soul region, and the mind, ego, and everything else is dependent on the soul. If the soul is withdrawn, nothing remains. Here also, if life is gone, the body will perish.

If the souls are withdrawn from this world, nothing will remain. The soul is reality. This mundane reality is to be described as a misconception which appears in the soul much the same as a dream appears in a person. The soul himself is unconcerned. And if the soul is returned to the world of soul, and consciousness is withdrawn from this plane, nothing remains. It is all darkness. And it cannot exist independently. So this material reality is created by the soul's revolting attitude, his unhealthy attitude.

Bishop Berkeley

Just as a man who is in a diseased condition experiences delirium. Disease is the cause of delirium. The delirium itself has no independent existence. The hallucination does not exist outside his mind. If you want to remove the delirium, you must treat the patient. His brain needs medicine. When he is treated, the world of delirium vanishes. In a similar way, the soul has developed a diseased condition, and he suffers from delirium. And as the collective souls are suffering collectively from this delirium, this world appears real. Collectively so many misguided delirious persons are being connected or disconnected with this material reality.

Dr. Murphey: Then what is the difference between the world of reality and the material world?

Śrīla Śrīdhar Mahārāj: This material world is only a reflection of complete reality; it is a conception we find exciting to us. Compelled by local interest of enjoyment, we have embraced this creation of the Lord. With our spiritual vision covered by the spectacles of prejudice, we are seeing things in a distorted way. The Lord is not to be blamed; our spectacles should be blamed. Everything is meant for Him; the only difference in our vision of reality is that our vision is tainted with the colors of our different kinds of selfish interests. And the different planetary systems in the material world are different sub-planes in the plane of enjoyment or exploitation. Our distorted consciousness is the source of the different colors of the things that surround us.

And when these illusory conceptions are fully removed, we will find that everywhere it is Krishna and Krishna only. And when the conception of Godhead as Lord and Master is removed, then receiving his impetus of activity from Krishna consciousness, the soul will find himself in Vṛndāvana. But in order to attain that stage, we must have no consciousness of this body, or the mind, or the country conception, the nation conception, or the globe conception. All planes of limited conception must be crossed. From soul to Supersoul, the soul must enter deeper and deeper into reality. You will find everything there. There you will find that Rādhārāṇī and Krishna in Vṛndāvana is not false. It is neither poetry nor imagination.

The only requirement is that we must develop our deeper nature, our self-identification, through self-determination. In Hegel's language, self-determination is the fulfillment of all of us. Self-determination in the Vaiṣṇava conception means *svarūpa-siddhi*, spiritual identity. Who am I? What is my deeper self beyond my mind or my intelligence? Where am I? What is my inner self-interest? I must enter the plane of reality, I must get back my proper self. And in Krishna's connection I will enter the environment and see what the world really is.

If I am given some wine or some poison, then I shall become beside myself. I shall see things in a distorted way. I will be unable to recognize my sister or mother, and actuated by animal nature, I will see everything as an object for my enjoyment. The crude tendency of lust will cover my vision of everything. Then again when I am sober, I shall see the same things, but my perception of them will be changed.

In this way we must be prepared to go deeper beneath the surface reality, and find out who we are, what is our real self-interest. We should try to see the paraphernalia of reality according to our genuine self-interest. Through self-determination we must learn to see things the opposite of the way we are seeing them at present. We must try to understand how to find ourselves. And by surrendering ourselves to Krishna's interest, then we shall try to go back home, back to Godhead.

A Floating World of Experience

There are many schools of atheist philosophers. The most famous atheist in Indian philosophy was Charvaka Muni. His philosophy is paralleled by the extreme atheists of Western philosophy. According to their opinion, consciousness is the by-product of the chemical combinations of different material substances. With the dissolution of this physical body, neither soul nor consciousness remains. Only the physical combination of the different elements of the body remain. Just as the combination of different chemicals produces something more than the individual chemicals themselves, the physical combination of different material elements produce consciousness. With the dissolution of this fleshy body, nothing remains. This philosophy was first propounded in the West by Epicurus.

Then there is Buddhism. The Buddhists say that when the physical body is dissolved, the subtle body, the mental system, goes on to take another birth. The Buddhists admit transmigration from one body to the next, or reincarnation. According to them, although this body may vanish, we must enter another body according to our *karma*. If we

Buddha

work in a particular way, then the subtle body, the mental system, dissolves, and nothing remains. According to the Buddhists, there is no soul.

Śaṅkarāchārya's philosophy is similar – with a slight difference. The Buddhist school says that the individual soul does not exist. According to them there is no permanent individual soul. Śaṅkarāchārya has also said that no permanent individual soul exists. But Śaṅkarāchārya says that conscious substance, Brahman, exists as the ultimate reality. This is the difference between Śaṅkarāchārya and the Buddhists. According to Śaṅkara, consciousness itself is true; it is only the consciousness of separate existence that is false. In his view the individual soul is only a reflection of the conscious substance which is the ultimate reality. With the dissolution of the mental system, each soul's consciousness of individuality vanishes; it is nonexistent in that ultimate plane of reality.

He gives the example of the moon and its reflection in a mirror. Remove the mirror and there is no reflection. His view is that all individual souls are reflections from a common source: Brahman, consciousness. So Śaṅkarāchārya says, in reality individual souls are one and the same with Brahman.

Śrī Chaitanya Mahāprabhu's interpretation of Vedānta is different from Śaṅkarāchārya's. Śrī Chaitanya says that we

Śaṅkarāchārya

have to accept the Vedic truth in its entirety, without any modification. Śaṅkarāchārya has accepted only a few Vedic aphorisms which constitute a partial representation of the truth. His four principle expressions taken from the *Vedas* are *ahaṁ brahmāsmi*: "I am Brahman"; *tat tvam asi*: "Thou art that"; *so'ham*: "I am that"; and *sarvaṁ khalv idaṁ brahma*: "Everything is Brahman." Śrī Chaitanya analyzed the meaning of the aphorism *sarvaṁ khalv idaṁ brahma* follows. According to Śaṅkarāchārya, everything is one. He says *brahma satyaṁ jagan mithyā*: Spirit is true, the world is false. Śaṅkarāchārya says that *brahma* (spirit) exists, and that *sarva* (everything) does not exist. If this is actually true, and everything is one, then why does the question of existence or nonexistence arise at all?

In the aphorism *sarvaṁ khalv idaṁ brahma, sarva* – everything – exists, and *brahma* – spirit – also exists In this expression, many exists and one also exists. There is many and there is one.

Again, if everything is one, then the question arises: to whom are we speaking? For whom have the *Vedas* come with this advice? Both the relative and the absolute exist together; they are coexistent. The absolute and the relative

Lord Śiva with Gaṅgamāyī (the Ganges) on his head.

are also represented in the Vedāntic aphorism *tat tvam asi*: Thou art that. *Tat* or "that" is there and *tvam* "you" is also there. Both variety and unity are found represented in the aphorism *tat tvam asi*, but Śaṅkarāchārya accepts one and rejects the other. His explanation is therefore a misinterpretation of the original meaning of the *Vedānta-sūtras*. It is not a proper interpretation of the *Vedas*, because he has thrust his own idea or conception forward in the name of the *Vedānta*. Śaṅkarāchārya's interpretation of *Vedānta* is artificial. It is selfish and provincial.

This is the refutation of Śaṅkarāchārya given by Śrī Chaitanya Mahāprabhu, and as far as we are concerned, it cannot be seen otherwise. If we try to follow the interpretation of Śaṅkarāchārya, then what meaning can be found in this statement of the *Upaniṣads: yato vā imāni bhūtāni jāyante yena jātāni jīvanti?* "The Absolute Truth is He from whom everything is coming, who is maintaining everything, within whom everything exists, and into whom everything enters at the time of annihilation." What does this mean? Does this statement say that the Absolute Truth is non-differentiated? It is sufficient for our understanding to accept its direct meaning. The self-explanatory meaning of these words is sufficient to understand this simple statement of the *Upaniṣads*.

Śrī Chaitanya Mahāprabhu defeats Śaṅkarāchārya through common sense. This is the unique characteristic of His argument. He defeats His philosophical opponents not with difficult, abstract, intellectual arguments, but with common sense.

When Śrī Chaitanya wanted to demonstrate the supremacy of Nārāyaṇa over Śiva, he said that one may just consider the position of the Ganges. The Ganges is the water that washes the feet of Nārāyaṇa, and yet she rests on the head of Śiva. From this, we can easily use common sense to see which of the two holds the superior position. When Śrī Chaitanya wanted to show that Krishna is greater than Nārāyaṇa, he pointed to the example of Lakṣmīdevī. She aspires after the association of Krishna. Although she has everything with Nārāyaṇa, still she has some aspiration for the company of Krishna. On the other hand the *gopīs* have no attraction for Nārāyaṇa. When they meet Nārāyaṇa, they pray that by His grace, their devotion to Krishna may be enhanced.

In this way, by applying common sense, intuition, we may judge the nature of reality. Intuition will be far more helpful than abstruse argument. *Vedānta* confirms this in the aphorism *tarko-pratiṣṭānat*: "Argument can never help us reach any real conclusion." Rather it is only intuition and common sense that can really help us. This is the recommendation of Śrī Chaitanya, and this is how He refuted many scholars including even the great all-conquering *digvijaya paṇḍita* of Kashmir.

Question: The Buddhists say that after one transcends sensory experience he will find that underneath it all there is actually no foundation of life. One will find that there's nothing there but the void. According to their teaching, after our experience is removed, there is no soul, no basis of existence. How do the Vaiṣṇava *āchāryas* deal with Buddhism?

Śrīla Śrīdhar Mahārāj: In South India, and especially in Andhra Pradesh, there are many Buddhist scholars. Śrī Chaitanya Mahāprabhu met the Buddhists when he was passing through South India. Chaitanya Mahāprabhu says *veda nā māniyā bauddha haya ta' nāstika*. Because the Buddhists do not accept the Vedic scriptures, they are considered atheists. Śaṅkarāchārya, in a hidden way, also preaches on behalf of the Buddhists. The difference between them is that Śaṅkarāchārya admits the existence of Brahman as the fundamental reality, whereas the Buddhists say that ultimately nothing exists.

The Vaiṣṇava *āchāryas* disagree with both Śaṅkarāchārya and with Buddha. They say that the *jīva* is an individual eternal soul. This particle of spiritual energy known as the *jīva* or spirit is tiny, like the dust particles of earth or the pencils-rays of the sun. There is the Supreme Infinite Soul or Consciousness, and the finite sparks of consciousness. Their relationship may be compared to the relationship between a

Descartes

great fire and the sparks that emanate from the fire. The sparks that emanate from the fire may become covered by darkness, but when they re-enter the shelter of that great conflagration, they are again perfectly situated.

To refute the atheism of the Buddhists, we may look to the modern European philosopher Descartes. Descartes said, "I doubt everything. Whatever you say, I doubt." Then, Descartes says, the question that arises is, "Does the doubter exist: true or false?" You have to start your search for truth from there. Who am I ? To whatever truth is related, whatever idea is stated, one may say, "I oppose that statement. I doubt it." Then the question arises does the doubter exist, or is he nonexistent? If he is nonexistent, then there can be no question of doubting. If one takes the position of an extreme skeptic, he must explain his own position. He may assert, "Whatever you have said, I doubt," but he must discern whether or not he really exists. That must be the starting point for any further inquiry.

And what is the doubter? Is he an atom? A particle of dust? Is he without knowledge? And if so, then how has he comes to assert doubt? This question should be examined. Whenever one may doubt, the question must be asked,

"Who is the doubter? Is he conscious? Does he have reason? Has he any existence at all? Or is he imaginary? Is it matter that is submitting the question? Or is a unit of consciousness asking the question? What is the origin of this question? Who is asking the question? Has it come from the conscious region? If it has, then what shall we consider as the basis of existence? Consciousness or matter? A fossil or God?"

Before the First World War, I was a student of law in the university. In my senior year I studied philosophy under a professor named Mr. Stevenson. He was a German scholar, but during the war he took Indian citizenship. His class dealt with ontology and psychology. Professor Stevenson's language was very simple, and he used fine arguments to make his point. He gave four arguments against atheism, one of which I find very useful: "Consciousness is the starting point of everything." Whatever you say presupposes consciousness. Any statement presupposes consciousness.

If we examine the fossil, what do we see? It is black, it is hard, it has some smell, some attributes, but what are these things? These are all different stages of consciousness. Without the help of consciousness, no assertion can be made. No assertion is possible at all. One may say that the fossil is the most elemental substance, but a fossil means what? Some color, sensation, hardness, taste; but the background is consciousness.

After everything is analyzed, we will find that it is an idea. This is Berkeley's theory. Everything is an idea in the ocean of consciousness. Just as an iceberg floats in the salt ocean, so the fossil is floating in the conscious ocean.

Ultimately everything – whatever we can assert, whatever is within the world of our experience – is floating like an iceberg in the ocean of consciousness. This point can never be refuted.

I have had personal experience of this. When I was twenty-three, I had some deep and natural indifference to the world. At that time I had an experience of the reality of consciousness. I felt the material world floating on consciousness just as cream floats on milk. Conscious reality is much deeper than the apparent reality of our present experience. The world of experience is like cream floating on milk which is the mind. This physical world is only the visible portion of reality floating over the mental world. I felt this myself. When there is a huge quantity of milk, the cream that floats over the milk and covers it is very meager. In the same way, I could feel at that time that this physical world is only a meager portion of reality, and that the subtle world, which is at present in the background, is far more vast. The mental world is a huge and vast reality, and the physical world is a small cover over that mental world.

Whatever can be perceived by the eye, the ear, the tongue, the nose, the skin – any of the external senses – is only a covering of reality. In *Śrīmad-Bhāgavatam,* Prahlāda Mahārāj says, *na te viduḥ svārtha-gatiṁ hi viṣṇuṁ, durāśayā ye bahir-artha-māninaḥ.* We are making too much of the covering of reality, we are devoting our minds to the external coating – *bahir-artha-māninaḥ* – but we do not dive deep into the eternal substance. If only we were to dive deep into reality, there we would find Viṣṇu. The most peaceful substance is within, but it is covered, just as milk is covered by cream, and we are making much of that cover. The real substance is within, just as fruit is covered by its skin. What we experience at present is the cover, the skin, and we are making much of that, ignoring the very substance which the cover is protecting.

The primary step in the search for truth is to penetrate the covering and find the knower within. And then begin our analysis. What is he? Is he an atom like an atomic particle of dust? Or is he a fantastic atom in the conscious plane? At first we must approach reality in this way. There is the knower and the unknown, the inquirer and the inquired.

Try to find yourself. Then gradually, you will come to know that you are the soul, the particle of consciousness within. And just as you are spirit covered by matter, the whole world is also like that; the spiritual reality within is covered. Upon realizing your self as spirit soul, you will be able to see that everything is a part of consciousness. Within the world of consciousness, worlds of different sorts of experience are floating. In the conscious sea, the sun, the moon, trees, stones, human beings, our friends, and our enemies are all floating. As we approach the spiritual plane, we will find it to be nearer to our real self. And in this way, we will see that matter is far, far away, but the soul is near.

Try to conceive of reality along these lines. Soul, spirit, consciousness, is nearer to the soul and you are a child of that soil. Matter is far, far away. But the interrupting planes are so close together that we don't see the nature of spiritual reality, just as if you put your hand over your eye, you can't see the hand. But if the hand is only one foot away, we can see it very clearly. Sometimes what is very close, we cannot see. I may be able to see so many things, but I cannot see myself.

Although the Buddhists and other atheists argue that consciousness is a material thing, I say that there is no material thing. If I am to answer the question of whether or not consciousness is produced from matter, then I shall say that nothing is material. Whatever we feel is only a part of consciousness. Everything is an idea. We are concerned only with consciousness from the beginning to the end of our experience. Beyond that we cannot go. Everything is an idea: the stone, the tree, the house, the body – all are ideas. The plane of consciousness is very much closer to us than we perceive. And what is shown as a particular thing is far away. We are involved only with ideas. We can't go outside that. Everything within our experience is a part of our mind.

Question: The *Purāṇas* say that there are 8,400,000 species of life. Are they only ideas?

Śrīla Śrīdhar Mahārāj: All ideas. Consciousness is always in the primary position. Yet these ideas are real, because they are also originally present in the spiritual reality Vṛndāvana. Nothing is eliminated in our conception of reality; everything is harmonious. Everything has its proper position; nothing is to be eliminated. The only thing necessary is harmony. Only our outlook, our angle of vision, needs to be changed. But in order to have that kind of vision, we must give up being self-centered. Both exploitation and renunciation must be given up. These two things cause this hallucination. Everything has its contribution to the service of the supreme Center, and if we can understand that, we become free from this relative world. The material world is a reflection of the spiritual world. There is undesirability here. From Brahmā, who holds the highest position in this universe, to the lowest creature *(ābrahma-bhuvanāl lokāḥ)*, everyone is prone to misconception. On the other hand, everything in Vṛndāvana contributes towards the pastimes of Rādhā-Govinda.

Everything in Vṛndāvana is Krishna conscious; every tree, creeper, and shrub. How can they be useless or ordinary shrubs and creepers? Uddhava is the greatest devotee of Krishna and he aspires to take birth as a creeper or a shrub in Vṛndāvana. What then, is the value of the shrubs and creepers of Vṛndāvana! Should we think that Uddhava's aspiration is imaginary or theoretical, with no practical value?

Everything in Vṛndāvana is necessary for the pastimes of Rādhā-Govinda. Everything in the spiritual environment has its indirect value. This is called *śānta-rasa*, or passive mellow. It may be understood in this way: if a man does not harm anybody, even a fly or a mosquito, that does not mean that he is paralyzed or diseased; he is simply in a passive mood. So in Vṛndāvana, service may be rendered in a passive mood. The Yamunā river, the trees the birds, and the insects, are absorbed in rendering service in a passive mood.

How this is so can be understood by the analogy of a drama. In a drama in the theater, an actor may play the part of a dead man. As his body is being carried, he can't say anything; he can't move. That does not mean that he is dead. Similarly, a devotee in *śānta-rasa* may assume a passive role as a creeper, a shrub, or a tree in Vṛndāvana, in order to enhance the drama of Rādhā-Govinda *līlā*.

Śrī Chaitanya Mahaprabhu

A devotee may also accept the role of a servant. He may be a king, but for the satisfaction of the Lord, he may play the part of a sweeper. While one is playing the part of a sweeper, he may perform his role so nicely that the men standing by applaud in appreciation. So the mood of servitude is also a contribution to the service of Krishna.

Another example of *śānta-rasa* is Rādhā-kuṇḍa. Rādhā-kuṇḍa, the bathing place of Śrīmatī Rādhārāṇī, where Krishna enacts his pastimes of conjugal love, is considered to be the highest place in Vṛndāvana. The gods and devotees all praise Rādhā-kuṇḍa. Should we think it to be an ordinary body of water? Rather, how exalted is the position of Rādhā-kuṇḍa.

Then there is Govardhana Hill. That is also a kind of pose. Apparently it is a hill, but Govardhana is worshiped as Krishna Himself. He also appears as a stone, as *śala-gram*; He appears in the form of the Deities.

Śrī Chaitanya Mahāprabhu prays, "O Lord, please consider me as the dust of Your holy feet," expressing Himself as a *vibhinnāṁśa jīva*. Foot-dust is generally inanimate. But when Chaitanya Mahāprabhu prays, "Consider me foot-dust," the dust He speaks of is not matter; it is a unit of consciousness filled with knowledge and love. The dust of the Lord's lotus feet is the emblem of knowledge and ecstasy. In the spiritual realm, existence and knowledge is presupposed. But more than that, the souls there are points of divine love in Vṛndāvana and Navadwīpa. And with the wholesale conversion of the souls of this world, everywhere we will find the kingdom of God. Krishna's kingdom, Mahāprabhu's kingdom, exists; we have only lost the proper angle of vision by which to see it. We must once again acquire that vision. At present we are in the midst of enemies, but if our angle of vision is changed, we shall think, "No, I am in the midst of friends."

And that angle of vision is so broad that one who sees in that way becomes fearless. When Jaḍa Bhārata was captured by dacoits and taken to the deity of Kālī to be sacrificed, his angle of vision was so spacious that he did not care for anything. He thought, "Whatever is happening is the Lord's will. He is the proprietor and witness of all. He sees everything. Everything is his will, and I have nothing to do with the outcome." With this idea, wherever Jaḍa Bhārata was taken, he went without resistance. Although he was about to be sacrificed, he was unconcerned. He thought, "I am in a friendly circle. There is no danger." He was in such a plane of consciousness that no apprehension, no danger, could affect him; he thought, "I am under Krishna's care." And so it is proved by Jaḍa Bhārata's practical example that this angle of vision is not simply philosophy or imagination. It is reality.

Krishna's divine will is in the background of everything that exists. And when one comes in connection with that paramount power, that original plane of reality, he will not have any care; he will become fearless, *māyā santuṣṭa-manasaḥ sarvāḥ sukha-mayā diśaḥ (Śrīmad-Bhāgavatam 11.14.13).*

Yet, in the plane of reality where Krishna is worshipped with knowledge-free devotion, *jñāna-śunya bhakti*, that sort of posing is there. There appears to be fear and concern, but that concern is quite different in nature from material cares. Influenced by *yogamāyā*, the *gopīs* and Krishna's friends want to know, "Krishna is not here! Where is He?" And in this way, the *gopīs* and cowherd boys run here and there searching for Krishna. Even the cows are concerned and stop grazing, but all this is conducted by *yogamāyā* for the satisfaction of Krishna. Such is the nature of *līlā* in the plane of *jñāna-śunya bhakti*.

We are engaged in an inner search for truth. And in the *Vedas* the answer to our questions, the essence of the whole revealed truth of the scriptures, can be summarized in one word, *oṁ*: "Yes!" What is the meaning of that "yes?" "What you want: yes, it exists. What you are searching for: yes, it is there! Your inner search to live and to improve will be fulfilled: seek and ye shall find." If you examine yourself and search out your innermost need, you will find that the revealed truth says, "Yes, your thirst will be quenched. You will be well-fed."

Question: In *Bhagavad-gītā*, Krishna says *jīva-bhūtāṁ mahā-bāho yayedaṁ dhāryate jagat:* the spiritual energy is sustaining this material world. How are we to understand this?

Śrīla Śrīdhar Mahārāj: The misguided souls of this world are from *taṭastha-loka*, the marginal plane, and misguided by misconception they have come within this illusory angle of vision.

Krishna says this world is dead matter. The souls entered here and movement came. They entered into this material conception and began moving it. In that sense, they are sustaining the universe, *yayedaṁ dhāryate jagat.* But ultimately everything is sustained by Him.

Krishna also says *ahaṁ sarvasya prabhavo:* "Everything emanates from Me." And in the *Vedas* it is said, *yato vā imāni bhūtāni jāyante.* He is the origin of everything in its creation, its maintenance, and its annihilation. But here in this material world, the fallen souls as so many sparks have entered like glowworms into the dark region showing the darkness surrounding it. The *jīva* souls are like glowworms in the dark night of this material world. Somehow they are carrying on in the darkness. We can barely trace them out as a meager light in the dark. They are almost completely covered by darkness, but still they can be distinguished. Spirit can know itself.

Question: Who did you say was expounding the atheist philosophy in the West?

Śrīla Śrīdhar Mahārāj: Epicurus is the greatest atheist of the West, as Charvaka Muni is in the East. According to Epicurus, with the dissolution of this physical body, nothing remains. And according to him there is no mental system; the mental system – what we come across in our dreams – does not have any separate existence. But Śaṅkara and Buddha both accept the existence of the mental system within the physical body. Transmigration of the soul is also admitted in their philosophy. But Buddha says that with the dissolution of the mental system – the *sukṣma śarira* – nothing remains.

Śaṅkarāchārya, on the other hand, says that the consciousness within the mental body is a reflection of Brahman, and Brahman is the ultimate existence. According to him, with the dissolution of the body, nothing remains but Brahman. Śaṅkarāchārya says:

śloka dhenu pravakṣyāmi
yad aktam yānti kotibhiḥ
brahma satyaṁ, jagan mithyā
jīva brahmaiva na paraḥ

Rāmānujachārya

"In half a verse, I am summarizing the truth that has been expressed by volumes and volumes of scripture. Within only half a verse I shall give the essence of all truths: *brahma satyaṁ, jagan mithyā.* Brahman, spirit, is true – this world is false. And the *jīva* is nothing but Brahman. This is the substance of all the scriptures."

Proper knowledge is not possible under the philosophical systems of Buddha and Śaṅkarāchārya. If what they say is true – the world is false – then we must ask, "Why do you speak? And to whom? If everything is false, is your philosophy also imagination?" We will have to ask Śaṅkarāchārya, "Does your coming to this world and your endeavor to refute Buddhism and establish oneness as the ultimate truth have no meaning? Who have you come to preach to? Why have you come to preach if this world has no reality? If this world is false, then why are you taking so much trouble to explain your philosophy? For what? Is your mission also imagination?"

The first great opponent of Śaṅkarāchārya was Rāmānuja. Rāmānuja's refutation was very strong and based on a sound foundation. Rāmānuja argued: "What is the necessity for Śaṅkarāchārya to endeavor with so much energy to establish his philosophy if it is all fictitious? To say, the world is false, is a suicidal position. Has he come here to do nothing? He has come to correct us and free us from error, but there must be errors. Error or misconception has reality, otherwise, what is the necessity of spending so much energy refuting so many propositions? *Māyā* exists. *Māyā* is eternal. The individual soul is eternal, and *māyā* is also eternal."

The basis of material existence is the possibility of the *taṭastha jīva* committing a mistake and developing misconception. The soul is *anu cetana*, atomic consciousness. And as atomic units of consciousness, our freedom is not perfect. Our defective freedom is the cause of this illusion. The soul must have freedom. Before a crime is committed, the possibility of committing a crime is present in the ordinary peace-loving subject. The possibility of disease is there, so hospitals, medicine, and special diets are all necessary. In the same way, the possibility for misconception is there in the soul because we are weak and limited.

Māyā, the world of measurement, is unnecessary for the Absolute, but necessary for those in the relative position. When there is only one self-interest, *māyā* is not necessary. But where there is division, differentiation, and distribution, when there are many ideas of self-interest, *māyā* is necessary.

Within the world of misconception, *māyā* is the law of the land. The law helps the law-abiding, and the law punishes the law-breaking. The law is the same for everyone; and that same law means protection for the good and suppression for the bad. Law means to divide rights. One and the same law provides for protection of the good and punishment of the bad. The *svarūpa-śakti*, the Lord's internal energy, helps the good, and the *māyā-śakti* punishes the bad.

Śakti, or energy, serves the purpose of the Lord, and therefore necessarily has two aspects, *paritrāṇāya sādhūnāṁ vināśāya ca duṣkṛtām*: to chastise the wicked and reward the good. When the Lord Himself appears, His purpose has two aspects: one for the good, another for the bad. He also comes here with that combined purpose. So although He is one, we see these two aspects of His character.

The conception that the unity of the absolute is not a stale, nondifferentiated thing is a theory that was propounded by Rāmānuja. This is called *viśiṣṭādvaita-vāda*, oneness with difference. The philosophy of Śaṅkarāchārya, on the other hand, is known as *kevalad-vaita-vāda*, exclusive oneness. Rāmānuja accepts that the Absolute Truth is one, but according to him, it is a differentiated oneness. He does not accept non-differentiated oneness. That it is one, he has no doubt. But that one is characterized by specification and differentiation. This is similar to the panentheism of Hegel.

Question: According to what you are saying, matter is also conscious because it is coming from the Lord who is the Supreme Consciousness. In the beginning, when we first differentiate between matter and spirit, we learn that matter is dead and the living entities manipulate it, but when we develop a higher realization will we see that matter is also living?

Śrīla Śrīdhar Mahārāj: Yes, and that is known as *śānta-rasa.* In a higher stage of realization we can detect consciousness everywhere: within glass, stone, earth, wood – in all the innumerable shapes and colors in which matter may appear.

We are always in the midst of consciousness. Consciousness is all-pervading, but is situated in different gradations of conception. The gradation of conception may differ, but it is all consciousness, all eternal: *paśu-buddhi-tanturājanam hariṣyeti.* We must try to reinstate ourselves in our own plane of reality. There, without the help of this mortal element, we can live happily. That transcendental plane is not a nondifferentiated world. It is not that there you have no individuality. If a nondifferentiated mass of consciousness can be admitted, then why should we not admit the existence of a system of consciousness? Rāmānuja says that it is a system. Śaṅkarāchārya says there is only a nondifferentiated mass of light-consciousness. Rāmānuja disagrees. He says that a differentiated light-mass of consciousness is the basis of reality. It is not undifferentiated or non-distinguishable.

And Śrī Chaitanya Mahāprabhu says that the basis of reality is *acintya bhedābheda*, inconceivable bipolarity. Everywhere there is something common and something different. Whatever opposing points you may discuss will have something in common, and something different. Nothing is quite the same as anything else. And above all, the infinite is not within your fist. It is inconceivable. The unified and differentiated character of reality is inconceivable; its secret is in the hand of the Supreme. It does not depend upon your whim. Still, that differentiated character of the Absolute will be seen differently according to the subjective relationship we have with Him.

An example of this is found in *Śrīmad-Bhāgavatam (10.43.17)*

> **mallānām aśanir nṛṇaṁ nara-varaḥ**
> **strīṇāṁ smaro mūrtimān**
> **gopānāṁ sva-jano 'satāṁ kṣiti-bhujāṁ**
> **śāstā sva-pitroḥ śiśuḥ**
> **mṛtyur bhoja-pater virāḍ aviduṣāṁ**
> **tattvaṁ paraṁ yogināṁ**
> **vṛṣṇīnāṁ para-devateti vidito**
> **raṅgaṁ gataḥ sāgrajaḥ**

"When Lord Krishna, accompanied by Baladeva, entered Kaṁsa's wrestling arena, He appeared to the spectators in different ways. Everyone viewed Him according to their own relationship (*rasa*) with Him. To the wrestlers He appeared as a lightning bolt. To the people in general He appeared as the most beautiful personality. To the ladies, He appeared to be the most attractive young man, Cupid personified, and thus increased their lust. The cowherd men looked upon Krishna as their own kinsman coming from the same village of Vṛndāvana. The kings who were present there saw Him as the most powerful ruler. His parents Nanda and Yaśodā saw Him as their most beloved child. Kaṁsa, the king of the Bhoja dynasty, saw Him as death personified. The worldly-minded saw Him as the Universal Form; the unintelligent saw Him as incapable, and to the yogis, He appeared to be the Supersoul. To the members of the Vṛṣṇī dynasty, He appeared to be their most celebrated descendant."

When Krishna entered the arena, everyone saw Him in their own way. In this way we can understand how He satisfies everyone. When Yaśodā sees Him, she says, "My boy!" But the *gopīs* see a grown-up – not a child. His friends see Him as one of their playmates. Krishna satisfies everyone. Even the animals in Vṛndāvana become ecstatic when they come in connection with Krishna.

barhāpīḍaṁ naṭa-vara-vapuḥ karṇayoḥ karṇikāraṁ
bibhrad vāsaḥ kanaka-kapiśaṁ vaijayantīṁ ca mālām
randhrān veṇor adhara-sudhayāpūrayan gopa-vṛndair
vṛndāranyaṁ sva-pada-ramaṇaṁ prāviśad gīta-kīrtiḥ

Śrīmad-Bhāgavatam 10.21 .5

"While the *gopīs* were describing the sweet vibration of Krishna's flute, they also remembered their pastimes with Him; thus their minds became enchanted, and they were unable to describe completely the beautiful vibrations. While discussing the transcendental vibration, they remembered also how Krishna dressed, decorated with a peacock feather on His head, just like a dancing actor, and with blue flowers pushed over His ear. His garment glowed yellow-gold, and He was garlanded with a *vaijayantī* garland made of *tulasī, kuṇḍa, mandāra, parījāta,* and lotus flowers. Dressed in such an attractive way, Krishna filled up the holes of His flute with the nectar emanating from His lips. So they remembered Him, entering the forest of Vṛndāvana, whose soil experiences the pleasure of consorthood upon being embraced by the touch of Krishna's lotus feet."

Krishna consciousness means full-fledged theism, up to consorthood. All conceptions of fulfillment are found there in their purest and most desirable position. This material world, however, is only a shadow, a black imitation of reality. Full-fledged theism means Krishna consciousness. In the full-fledged conception of theism, the Infinite embraces the whole of the finite. It comes down to completely embrace and welcome the finite. This kind of full-fledged theism is found in Vṛndāvana. There, one negligent part of the finite may find the bliss of the embrace of the whole of the Infinite. In Vṛndāvana, not a corner of the finite is left unfulfilled; every particle of sand and every creeper is well-represented there, with complete personality in the loving pastimes of Śrī Krishna.

Here in this material world, however, a particle of sand is nothing; it is ignored. But there, everything is well-attended. In Vṛndāvana there is no ignorance. No interest of anything is ignored there; everything is harmonized, and therefore the conception of Vṛndāvana in Krishna consciousness is the highest conception of full-fledged theism. *Śrīmad-Bhāgavatam* says, "Whenever Krishna sets his lotus feet within Vṛndāvana, the Earth personified says, 'My fate is fulfilled, I have achieved my highest fortune.' In Vṛndāvana, the earth, the very dust, feels the pleasure of the highest type of conjugal love merely by the touch of His lotus feet. Wherever Krishna puts his footsteps, the Earth's joy knows no bounds. By his touch, the Earth feels the most intense type of ecstasy.

In Vṛndāvana, Krishna is *mādhurya*, sweetness personified. He is *ānanda*, ecstasy personified. And Krishna responds to our own inner demands in every way. The Supreme Center has the peculiar capacity of responding to all our needs and satisfying the thirst of all existence. According to their capacity, rank, and dignity Krishna distributes to all souls the juice from the sweet sea of transcendental mellow, *yo yaṁ śraddhā sa eva saḥ.*

One can taste the sugar-candy sweetness of the Absolute, according to one's capacity, just as sugar candy is tasted in different ways. For a normal tongue sugar candy is very sweet, but if there is a boil on the tongue even sugar candy is bitter.

When a man is working, his manager will see him as a worker; his child will see him as a father, and his wife will see him as a husband. His servant will see him as master. Dogs and other animals will view him in another way. The same person will be seen differently according to the relationship between seer and seen. Similarly, Krishna appears differently to those who view him according to their respective *rasa*. In this way, the differentiated character of the Absolute is revealed according to the soul's subjective qualifications.

Thesis, Antithesis, & Synthesis

Śrīla Śrīdhar Mahārāj: What subjects are you studying?

Student: Philosophy and religion.

Śrīla Śrīdhar Mahārāj: In which university?

Student: San Francisco State.

Śrīla Śrīdhar Mahārāj: You are a student of religion and philosophy. Have you studied Hegel? Hegel's philosophy is sometimes described as panentheism. Panentheism proposes that God is present in all things, but in contrast to pantheism it affirms that God is also an independent being above and beyond all things. Hegel is also known for Perfectionism. He says that the nature of the Absolute is both conditioned and unconditioned combined. The truth develops through thesis, antithesis, and synthesis, and by this method everything progresses. According to Hegel, the Absolute is by Itself and for Itself. And he also used the German equivalent of the expression "die to live." These were his chosen expressions.

Such expressions are very useful for those in the theistic line. If you want to live a progressive life you will have to

George Wilhelm Friedrich Hegel

die as you are. Your ego must be dissolved and then the real inner or finer self will come out. This is a good philosophy to have appeared amongst the Westerners. The concept of die to live comes in the line of Vaiṣṇavism. Hegel has also said that the Absolute is "by Himself" and "for Himself." "For Himself" means that the Absolute Truth is the Supreme Enjoyer. In the *Bhagavad-gītā* Krishna says:

ahaṁ hi sarva-yajñānāṁ
bhoktā ca prabhur eva ca
na tu mām abhijānanti
tattvenātaś cyavanti te

This is the most vital point to establish God as a person. He is the enjoyer. If anything is enjoyed, the enjoyer will hold the supreme position. This cannot but be. Everything is meant for His enjoyment. And He is the supreme. "By Himself" means that the absolute is supreme – everything is meant for His satisfaction. This is a necessary truth; it is not questionable. And also, His existence is subjective.

No object can exist without a subject. No thing can exist without a thinker. There must be a thinker. For example, what is a fossil? As we examine it we observe color and the hardness of stone, but these qualities are simply thoughts within us – a thinking stage. What is color? A concept within our consciousness. So any kind of existence presupposes a subject or consciousness. This is the crux of the argument. No object can exist without a subject. And no subject can exist without an object. There is the thinker and the thought. If there is a thinker, he must be thinking something – so an object is there. And if there is an object, then whatever attribute it has must be reflected in the consciousness of a subject. Otherwise no existence is possible. Do you follow?

Student: Yes. It is very clear.

Śrīla Śrīdhar Mahārāj: These are all Hegel's original conceptions, his contributions to philosophy. He was a very important philosopher. And for a Western thinker, his philosophy was very near to that of the Eastern thinkers. In many respects, Hegel's philosophy is very close to Rāmānuja's philosophy.

Of course, there are many important Western philosophers. Kant's philosophy is very influential. Are you familiar with Kant?

Student: Yes.

Śrīla Śrīdhar Mahārāj: Have you studied Descartes?

Student: Yes, somewhat. He said, "I think, therefore I am."

Śrīla Śrīdhar Mahārāj: He is said to be the father of modern philosophy. Then there is Berkeley: he is an extreme subjective thinker. Locke, Hume, Mill, Berkeley, Johnson, Kant, Hegel – all these are important Western philosophers.

Student: I prefer to study Eastern philosophy.

Śrīla Śrīdhar Mahārāj: What kind of Eastern philosophy do you study? Sāṇkhya? Yoga? Nyāya? Vaiśeṣika?

Student: Zen Buddhism and Taoism – Chinese philosophy.

Śrīla Śrīdhar Mahārāj: Confucius came from China. Before Buddhism, Confucius was present in China. Then gradually moving West we find Socrates, Plato, and Aristotle. Have you studied them?

Student: Yes, I have studied them a little.

Śrīla Śrīdhar Mahārāj: The concept of Parallelism forwarded by Plato is also accepted in Vaiṣṇava philosophy to a certain extent. According to Plato, the forms we experience are a reflection of ideal form. This was his understanding of how the forms we perceive are a perverted reflection of the original spiritual world. That is the theory of Parallelism of Plato.

Student: Can you please explain more about the parallels between Hegel's philosophy and Krishna consciousness?

Śrīla Śrīdhar Mahārāj: In Hegel's philosophy, truth progresses through thesis, antithesis, and synthesis. The truth moves in a crooked way. In the philosophy of Krishna consciousness, the word *vilāsa* means "playful movement."

Plato

You may take it to mean that the Absolute is absorbed in play. And that is expressed through crookedness. *Aher iva gatiḥ premnaḥ svabhāva-kuṭilā bhavet:* A serpent moves in a crooked way; similarly, the movements of the Absolute are not straight, but crooked. *Vilāsa,* or the conception of *līlā* – the divine pastimes of the Lord – is something like that. This is similar to Hegel's opinion in which the truth develops in a crooked way through thesis, antithesis, and synthesis. There is thesis, then its opposite, and then again they unify and create a new thesis. Then again antithesis, and again a greater harmony in synthesis.

In this way truth is dynamic; it develops and makes progress. Hegel was the deepest thinker among the Western philosophers. Of course, other German scholars like Max Muller were also deep thinkers. In fact, Germany had such great appreciation and fondness for Indian culture that certain ancient books that can no longer be found in India may still be found in Germany. The Germans were never the colonial masters of India, but still they were extremely inquisitive to know about the cultural books of India. In spite of the war, many rare, ancient Indian books that can no longer be found in India are still safely preserved in Germany.

Student: I had a question regarding the philosophy of Berkeley. According to Berkeley the world is in the mind. It seems that the Berkeley theory tends to negate the existence of this world. It tends to argue against any type of reality.

Śrīla Śrīdhar Mahārāj: But Hegel has come to relieve Berkeley somewhat. Someone may challenge Berkeley: "I may think that there is a hundred dollars in my pocket, but if I search my pocket, will I find it there?" Hegel says that it must be there somewhere in the Universal Mind. That is Hegel's standpoint.

Student: Then it is present somewhere.

Śrīla Śrīdhar Mahārāj: And that wave comes gradually. This was my argument regarding Bhaktivinoda Ṭhākur's *Jaiva Dharma*. Have you read that book?

Student: No, I'm not familiar with that book.

Śrīla Śrīdhar Mahārāj: In that novel, the characters who speak on spiritual life are apparently imaginary. The different persons in that book – Brajanātha, the Bābājī, and others – seem to be imaginary characters discussing spiritual life. But I once explained that what is in Bhaktivinoda Ṭhākur's mind, what he has written in *Jaiva Dharma*, is not imagination. At one time or other, the persons and events he mentions must have existed, and these things will again have to come into existence. Do you follow?

Student: I'm not sure.

Śrīla Bhaktivinoda Ṭhākura

Śrīla Śrīdhar Mahārāj: What Bhaktivinoda Ṭhākur saw in his mind must exist somewhere in this world, sometime in the future, or sometime in the past. That very thing he describes in an apparently fictional way actually existed. Let me give you an example. When I speak, the sound moves at a certain speed. That sound can be heard later in another place. The same is true in the case of light, isn't it?

Student: Yes.

Śrīla Śrīdhar Mahārāj: So Śrī Chaitanyadeva, with his divine sound, chanted here and performed *saṅkīrtana*. He preached and the velocity of that divine wave is still going on. And now in some place in a universe, it may be found. Do you follow? Am I clear?

Student: I think so.

Śrīla Śrīdhar Mahārāj: The velocity of that light is going on; it is not lost. In the same way, the sounds I am now pronouncing are not lost; they are traveling for some distance through time and space. Whatever I see, that wave of light, is also traveling. The radio broadcasts from World War II – that war period, the war vision – is also there in space somewhere, vibrating at a certain rate. That vibration was once here, but now it somewhere else. It is floating in some plane of reality in time and space. If I throw a flower into the waters of the Ganges, then it is carried away by the current. If I can move with more speed than the current, I can find that flower somewhere else far away in the river. So the velocity of light – eyesight velocity – moves 186,000 miles in a second. If it is possible to move faster than the speed of light, then we can overtake the wave of visual events that are carried by that light. It is possible.

In a similar way, what exists in the plane of imagination now must have existed in reality at some time in the past or future, but it is now found somewhere else. It is said that the pastimes of Krishna move from one universe to the next in the same way that the sun moves from one time zone to the next. Now morning is here; five minutes from now, sunrise and morning will take place somewhere else. In this way, it is always sunrise somewhere. Here or there, the rising sun is to be found somewhere on the Earth. If we can move at the speed of the sun, then for us it will always be sunrise.

What came within the mind of Bhaktivinoda Ṭhākur, what he may have described in an apparently fictional way, must exist somewhere in the plane of reality, in the past or in the future. It is reality, not imagination.

Everything is real. It is not imagination. What I see in my dreams is now false. But in some former lifetime, in my past I experienced that reality. I had that sort of vision, and that has come to me now as a dream. It was a fact, and only now is it a dream.

What is in the mind may be abstract to us, but in the Universal Mind, everything is concrete. Whatever exists within the plane of imagination must be, and can be traced somewhere.

Student: Although everything is, in one sense, in the mind, still, when I feel hot and I find that others also feel hot, I conclude that it is hot. It seems that according to Berkeley, this is just going on in my mind.

Śrīla Śrīdhar Mahārāj: You have to understand the fundamental truth that what is hot to you may be a cold environment for some other organism. It is a question of degree. Our experience of coolness and heat depends on our degree of tolerance. What is cool to us may be hot to another. In this way we have to adjust with the idea of reality; what is hot to me may be cool to another. Reality is one thing for human beings; it is something else entirely for insects, worms, and other organisms. What is bright to us is dark to another. What is bright to an owl is dark to us. Do you follow?

Student: Yes.

Śrīla Śrīdhar Mahārāj: Creation is of a variegated nature. The experience of our eyes and ears is different from the experience of others whose senses are different from ours. What we can hear, others cannot hear. But our ears cannot detect subsonic or ultrasonic sounds. Our ears can detect only a limited spectrum of sound. Our vision is also limited. We can see neither infrared nor ultraviolet light. Our feeling, our sense of touch, is sensitive to an extremely limited degree. So all realities are co-existent; reality is adjusted according to our own experience. Something feels cool to me; that very thing is hot to another. In this way it is "hot" or "cold" according to our subjective experience. And so "our reality" will exist. So what is perceived by the mind is not imagination; it is reality. What is imagination to me is reality to another. The rising sun and the setting sun can be perceived simultaneously from different angles of vision. Within the whole creation all experience is co-existent.

What you now feel to be cool you can easily feel to be very hot by the will of the Supreme Lord. By His will, everything is possible. Everything depends on Him. He is the ultimate cause. What you consider as intolerably hot, you will be forced to feel as intolerably cold in a minute, if God so wills it. Everything depends upon His will. And that is coming here in either a modified way, in a general way, or in a particular special way according to His whim. In this way there may exist a gradation in how He manifests His will, but His will is the prime cause of everything. And He is above law. We must be conscious of that. Then we will be able to explain anything.

Student: So He is something like a hypnotist.

Śrīla Śrīdhar Mahārāj: Yes, He is a hypnotist. Everything depends on the sweet will of the Absolute. Everything is designed and destined by Him. Everything is in His hands.

The absolute center is by Himself and for Himself. He alone knows the purpose of everything. No one else. He alone knows His ways; no one else can know His ways. We may know only as much as He wants us to know. And that also can change by His sweet will. So He is completely free, an autocrat.

And that supreme autocrat can be captured only by love, not by knowledge. His ways are uncertain. How will our knowledge help us to understand Him ? Knowledge may be useful in understanding a thing if it follows a fixed law and has a fixed nature. But the Absolute is an autocrat; at any moment He can change all the laws. Then how shall we know the Infinite? In trying to understand the Absolute Truth, all our previous experience becomes null and void. At every second He can show us a new color. No degree of knowledge can make any clear statement of truth about God. Knowledge is futile in regard to the Infinite. First He is moving in one way, then another. On what basis will we make our calculation? His position is always changing by His sweet will.

His heart can be captured only by surrender. Through surrender alone we may please Him. And if He likes, He may make Himself known to us, but even then we may only know that portion of His personality, only that much about Him, that He cares to reveal to us. The designer of reality is an autocrat; He is above law. We must consider this carefully. He who is designing this universe is above law. He is not under the jurisdiction of any law. He does not have any fixed nature. At any time,

He may change His position according to His sweet will. And whatever He wills, that must come about.

Student: Bertrand Russell says that if there is a God, He must not be good. God Himself is not bound by law, but if we violate the law of God, we suffer. If God were good, He could have created all the souls of this world above law.

Śrīla Śrīdhar Mahārāj: If he says that, then that means that he wants to become the God of Gods. To Mr. Russell we say, "The Absolute Truth is unknown and unknowable. How can His ways be known? He is an autocrat. And you want to impose your crooked, meager, finite experience upon the Universal Truth! Your experience is the limited of the limited. And you want to thrust that small experience onto the unlimited whole? It is a most deplorable argument based on an assertion of faulty knowledge. From your finite position you want to know the measure of the whole Infinite, and then criticize Him. What is the foundation of your criticism? From what basis are you approaching the Infinite to criticize Him? How much do you know about Him?

"If you see a mother chastising her son, and you see only that portion of her behavior, you may conclude that she is very cruel. But you do not know the affection with which the mother cares for the child. You are not aware of how she feels for his future good. You are unaware of all this. You may say that she is punishing the son and that she is therefore cruel, but you do not know the context of her behavior. Every incident must have its future and its past, and you must carefully trace that out before passing any judgment or making any remark.

"In your case, how much are you limited in relationship to the Infinite? To what extent can you understand Him? Your capacity for knowing the Infinite is very meager. No one should attempt to make any remark about the infinite will on the basis of his own limited capacity. That is injudicious, and suicidal to a man of understanding."

Student: I have heard it said that according to Vedic ontology, the soul is marginal. Do the *jīva* souls in the marginal or *taṭastha* position have knowledge that there is an upper and a lower world, that there is suffering in the material world and divine service in the spiritual world?

Śrīla Śrīdhar Mahārāj: A *jīva* soul has adaptability of both sides; marginal means "endowed with adaptability towards both the spiritual and material worlds without participation or any experience of either." The marginal soul (*taṭasthā-jīva)* has only seed adaptability towards both. He is situated in the margin between the spiritual and material worlds, and the margin strictly means that one is in a position to analyze adaptability. He can go towards the spiritual world and he can come towards the material world. The possibility of either is there in potentiality, but he is left to exercise his freedom. Because the soul is a conscious unit, he has free will. Freedom is inseparable from consciousness. A conscious unit and freedom are one and the same. Conscious atom means endowed with freedom. Without freedom, it is matter.

Student: The soul has freedom, but does it have knowledge of the different aspects of reality?

Śrīla Śrīdhar Mahārāj: Because the soul is very small, his freedom is also imperfect; a soul in the marginal position is very vulnerable. Freedom does not mean absolute freedom. Because the soul's existence is small, his freedom is defective; there is the possibility of committing a mistake. Freedom of the minute soul does not mean perfect freedom. Complete freedom would be perfect reality, but the minute soul is endowed with the smallest atomic freedom. This is the position of the atoms of consciousness, and this is why they are vulnerable. They may judge properly or improperly; that is the position of those who are situated in the marginal position. If the soul were not endowed with the freedom to determine his position, we would have to blame God for our suffering. But we cannot blame God. The starting point of the soul's suffering is within himself.

The suffering of the soul in bondage is similar to the suffering of one who is addicted to a drug. Before one begins taking intoxication, the first step towards addiction is curiosity. Then after one has taken intoxication for a certain amount of time, he cannot do without intoxication. Our attachment to *māyā*, or misconception, is like addiction to a drug. At first we are curious, but when we become habituated to the intoxication of misconception, we are forced to continue using that intoxicating substance. Before beginning the habit it might never have begun. But once you have begun, as much as you cultivate an addiction, the intoxication will devour you.

The first cause of our entanglement with material nature was our mixing with *māyā* in a play of curiosity. But as much as we make friends with her, so much she comes to devour us. In this way we are in the clutches of *māyā*. But in the beginning our involvement was very slight, like one experimenting with drugs. The beginning of our play with *māyā* involved the voluntary misuse of our free will, and that has led us to this present stage where *māyā* has devoured us. *Māyā* means our attraction for intoxication: where there is love of exploitation, there is *māyā*. And truth is the opposite of exploitation. Truth is found in dedicating everything for the center, for Krishna.

Student: If in the marginal position *(taṭasthā)* the soul has exposure to both reality and illusion, why doesn't he have enough discrimination to come to the right path?

Śrīla Śrīdhar Mahārāj: He has no real depth of discrimination; only a little discrimination. But it is there. However small it may be, it is there.

Student: Can he also go to the spiritual domain of the Lord?

Śrīla Śrīdhar Mahārāj: Yes, and some souls do go to that side. Some go to that side, and some come to this side. The soul has independence. Not all come to one side or the other. Then there would be some compulsion. But there is no compulsion. It is a free choice; some are coming to this side, and some are going to that side.

Student: Is there any knowledge that can come from outside, or is it possible for the soul in the marginal position to get help from an outside agent?

Śrīla Śrīdhar Mahārāj: At every stage in our existence, outward help is present. But in the undifferentiated stage of spiritual existence in the marginal plane, only higher agents can help. An ordinary saintly person cannot detect the defects or transcendental qualities in the undifferentiated soul. Such help is the work of a higher personality. Only God Himself or an exalted or empowered saintly person can help a soul in that condition. Suppose you have a newborn baby. Only a doctor who is a specialist with advanced knowledge can treat the newborn. But when the child is a little grown up and can talk, he can explain the symptoms of what is paining him. At that time, an ordinary doctor may help him. Ordinary saints cannot help us in every stage of life. They can guide us and help us only up to a certain standard. But the Lord Himself and those highly empowered saints who are closely connected to Him can help us in any stage of our spiritual development.

The Super Subject

Question: How can we apply proper discrimination and judgment in our search for knowledge of the Infinite?

Śrīla Śrīdhar Mahārāj: Discrimination may take place in different planes, but it must have a connection with the higher plane. Judgment and discrimination should be in the right plane. Judgment and discrimination come from our side, but our progress depends on the favor of the higher side. It must have that connection, so surrender is required. Then the Lord will approach us and take us up to that higher plane. Somehow, we have to persuade the highest authority to favor us. We must invite the higher authority to accept us. It does not depend so much on our own ability, but on our submission and surrender, our hankering for mercy – not our positive capacity but our negative character, our surrender. As a subject, I cannot make the Infinite the object of my discrimination; He is always the super-subject. I cannot make God the object of my discrimination. He is super-subjective. My position, my attitude, must invite the higher authority to come down to my level and help me, favor me. Real discrimination or knowledge

1/19/2021 1:15pm

should take us to self-surrender. Surrender is necessary to attract the attention of the Lord. Everything depends on His sweet will. He is an autocrat: His sweet will is everything. To attract His sweet will, to increase our negative side, our tendency for surrender, to attract His favor, this will be our real problem if we wish to progress in spiritual life. And to attract the Lord's attention, all our qualifications must be of a negative character: we shall require surrender, submission, humility. And then we can press our position by praying, "O my Lord, I'm in the worst need; without Your grace I can't stand. I am helpless. I cannot endure without Your favor." That sort of hankering, earnestness, and necessity for His mercy will help us. In other words, we are to improve our negative character, and in that way we shall attract the positive, Krishna.

Then we shall develop proper discrimination, for at that time our subjective character will be to act only as His agent. He will inspire from within in whatever we do. Our discrimination will be utilized in carrying out His order. It will not be possible for us to have any separate interest, any original discrimination. I will carry out His order, or the order of the higher officer of the Supreme Lord. I may use my discrimination about how to make the lower arrangements in carrying out that order. But towards the Lord, who is higher than me, my attitude will always be one of submission, surrender, obedience, allegiance, unconditional slavery. The slave mentality will help us in entering that plane. If we truly feel ourselves to be low and in want, then the supply of mercy will come from the higher plane. This should always be the tenor of our thought: high and low. Subjective and objective. And Krishna is not subject to any rule; He is an autocrat. These are the data we must keep in our mind always. Everything moves according to His sweet will; our problem, then, is how to draw His attention. This will be possible only by increasing our negative tendency, by proving to Him, in a bona fide way, that I'm the most needy. At that time, we shall develop proper discrimination and knowledge; that is, our discrimination will be utilized in carrying out His order.

Question: In the *Īśopaniṣad*, there is a mantra:

> **vidyāṁ cāvidyāṁ ca yas**
> **tad vedobhayaṁ saha**
> **avidyayā mṛtyuṁ tīrtvā**
> **vidyayāmṛtam aśnute**

The translation has been given by Śrīpāda Bhaktivedānta Swāmī Mahārāj as follows: "Only one who can learn the process of nescience and that of transcendental knowledge side by side can transcend the influence of repeated birth and death, and enjoy the full blessings of immortality." What does he mean by learning the process of nescience and that of knowledge side by side?

Śrīla Śrīdhar Mahārāj: One is negative and another is positive. Knowledge means to know what is false and to leave that, and to recognize what is true and to accept that. Do you follow? To cultivate an understanding about falsehood and truth means to know, "This is false, we must reject it; this is truth, I must accept it." In that way this verse may be understood. To know the bad, to culture the bad, means to know when a thing is bad and to reject it, and to culture the truth means to accept it. Not that culture means that we should culture ignorance in order to have it. What is encouraged here in this mantra is rejection of falsehood and acceptance of truth. The defects of *māyā* should be analyzed. We must know: "Oh, this is *māyā*. This is bad, this is hopeless, this is undesirable." We must know to avoid these things. We must reject nescience and we shall try to attain science, knowledge. We shall try to understand the bright side and aim for the light, to accept it more and more and progress towards truth.

Question: A fifteenth century German Catholic philosopher, Nicholas of Cusa*, taught the doctrine *Of Learned Ignorance.* How would that compare to Vaiṣṇava philosophy?

Śrīla Śrīdhar Mahārāj: We may accept the bright side: noble ignorance in our view is *jñāna-sunya bhakti*, knowledge-free devotion. Noble ignorance means not to

---

* The *Dictionary of Philosophy* contains the following entry: "**Nicholas of Cusa** (or **Nicholas Cusanus**) (c. 1400—64) German cardinal, whose "*theological negativa*" was influential in the Renaissance. Main philosophical work: *De Docta Ignorantia* (Of Learned Ignorance) (1440). Using the methods of medieval logic, Cusanus examined the nature of God (Book I) and the Universe (Book II). His view of their relationship was fundamentally Neoplatonic; the Universe (*maximum contractum*), seen as the totality of finite things, flows out from and returns to God (*maximum absolutum*), whose nature is unknowable. Hence all human knowledge is simply learned ignorance.

attempt to calculate in this world but to surrender: to lose our faith in calculation, in our subjective capacity of calculation, and to surrender to the Supreme. We may interpret *jñāna-sunya bhakti* like that. "Learned ignorance" is when learning understands its own limit, when one realizes, "I'm finite, my learning is also finite; learning cannot make me a bona fide inquirer about the Infinite." It is better to surrender to the Infinite, and let Him work within us for our best interest. Submission, surrender to the Infinite, is the highest reach of learning. Learned ignorance means to realize that we can't know the Infinite. If he makes Himself known to us, then we can know Him; otherwise not.

Question: Nicholas of Cusa said, "God is inconceivable by thought." What do you say?

Śrīla Śrīdhar Mahārāj: Yes, only through devotion and by His grace may God be known. Our cultivation of knowledge won't give us God. That is the failure of knowledge – investigation about God, the Infinite. Only His grace can give Him. We have to come to the side of devotion and do away with knowledge. Our attempts to make much of knowledge will be stopped when coming in connection with the Infinite. Knowledge has got its limit. And when knowledge fails, faith begins. Knowledge fails and faith develops. You must develop faith and give up hope in knowledge. A research laboratory cannot give you God. When the Russian cosmonaut Yuri Gagarin returned from space, an old lady inquired from him: "You went so high; have you seen God there?" But he was an atheist.

He said, "God is like a horse drawing our cart. What do you think about God for? We use God in our service. With our knowledge and our research science we have forced God to serve us." This is the proud boast of science: "We have engaged God in our service; we are above God, superior to God. God is our creation." As if He is the creation of a particular half-mad section of society.

Question: Nicholas of Cusa also taught that "in God, opposites coincide. Opposites – smallest and greatest – come together in God." What is your understanding?

Śrīla Śrīdhar Mahārāj: Not only big and small, but even good and bad, even anti-parties, everything is harmonized in God. Good-bad, friend-enemy, everything is harmonized and accommodated there. And they lose their poison; all become good. He is the all-accommodating, all-harmonizing, all-adjusting principle, both directly and indirectly. Thesis and antithesis find their highest synthesis in the Krishna conception of divinity.

Science vs. NeScience

Student: I have finished my studies and now I am taking a break, a vacation.

Śrīla Śrīdhar Mahārāj: Please don't take offense, but that you are involved in the present system of education means that you are diving deeply in the ocean of ignorance. You are making progress in the ocean of ignorance.

Student: What do you mean by that?

Śrīla Śrīdhar Mahārāj: As a student of nescience you are moving in the opposite direction from truth. You are being taught that you and other souls of your type are the subjects, the center of the universe, and everything, all else, is an object meant only for your exploitation. You are being taught that we are exploiters and that the entire environment is for our exploitation. That is the foundation upon which the present system of education is based – a conception which is completely false.

In reality, we are not the subject, the center of the universe. The cause is in the higher world. Krishna is the Supreme Absolute Truth. Simply by His will, everything is brought into existence. He said, "Let there be light," there was light; "Let there be water," there was water; "Let there be earth," there was earth. His will is all-powerful. To know this is real education – subjective learning. What we experience sprang up from the divine will. Just as if He were a magician, He can show one thing to you and something entirely different to me. The Supersubject, the universal subject, has such power. So our idea is completely the opposite of the fossilists. It is not that from time eternal the fossil is developing into this world of experience – it is just the opposite. Therefore, by conceiving of this world on the basis of fossilism, we are diving deep into an intense ocean of ignorance.

Bhaktivedānta Swāmī Mahārāj asked a few of his disciples who were research scholars to crush the fossilism of Darwin, that is, the idea that everything is coming from fossils. This idea must be demolished. It is not so.

Everything is coming from above. What we experience at present is like the outcome of hypnosis. In the process of hypnosis, the hypnotist can make us withdraw our consciousness from anything at any moment and show us another way to view reality. In the same way, Godhead is free, and whatever He wills becomes reality. Whatever he imagines becomes reality *(satya-sankalpa).* He can force us to see something, and when He does so, we cannot see it in any other way.

If you can understand this principle, you can understand how everything is possible with divinity. Then you can have some faith in what is Godhead. Godhead means this:

the origin of creation. And yet this creation is only an insignificant part of His divine nature. He has infinite qualities and activities. And this world in which we live is only a negligible part of the cosmic manifestation. The whole basis of everything is there in Him. It comes from up to down, and not from down to up. To the idea that everything is developing from downward to up we must say, "no." A fossil is not a thing perfect or sufficient enough to create all this. To say that from a fossil intelligence is coming is a fool's conception.

Intelligence can be traced everywhere. As much as we analyze, we find higher reason, higher intelligence. Scientists are astonished to find the intelligence that is within nature. They continue to discover higher and higher laws. And yet all those laws already existed. It is just that these fools had no awareness of it, but an extremely fine degree of order existed long before their "discovery." The wonderful laws of nature existed long before their invention. And this is evident everywhere. The physical laws of nature do not exist by dint of their creation. Do the scientists create the laws of nature? They may invent so many things, but the intelligence within nature already exists. And there is something more: Power exists everywhere. Where has it come from? The scientists, intelligence to discover or invent a thing: where has it come from? Is it coming from the brain? Or is it merely a portion of dead flesh? Does intelligence come from somewhere else?

Consciousness, spirit, is all-pervading. It is present even in the trees, stones, earth, ether, air, everywhere. And to know the truth, we must connect with the conscious principle of the infinite. What is the Infinite? He is almighty, omniscient, omnipotent, all sympathetic, all-loving. Our real aspiration must be to have a direct connection with Him, leaving aside the charm of His created substance. We should want to negotiate how we can have a connection with the Creator Himself.

And His position is not simply that of creator. This world is a creation of a lower order. But a higher creation also exists in a plane of reality which is infinitely higher than this world of experience. We should inquire whether it is possible for us to have a life in that soil. We should try to understand what are the layers of reality in that realm of consciousness, and how we can go higher and higher in that plane. We should inquire about that and find out how we can enter there. We must try to understand what is the key to the entrance into that transcendental abode. This should be the basis of our search for truth. We should inquire into how to become free from both the plane of renunciation and the plane of exploitation.

Once, Krishna went to the court of the Kauravas, the camp of Duryodhana and Dhṛtarāṣṭra, with talk of peace. At that time, Karṇa, Duryodhana, and the others in the party attempted to bind Him down and put Him into prison. They thought that if Krishna were to be imprisoned, then the whole Pāṇḍava camp would automatically be finished. They knew that Krishna was the life and soul as well as advisor of their enemies, the Pāṇḍavas. They thought, "Now we have Krishna in our fist; we must immediately imprison Him." They went to tie Him down, but Krishna manifested His Universal Form. At that time, He revealed His divine nature in such a way that the men who went to tie Him down were perplexed. They thought, "What is He!" When Krishna manifested His Universal Form of thousands of heads, hands, and legs, they thought, "This is a gigantic thing! Here in this form we find Bāladeva on one side, Arjuna on another, and Bṛghu on another. Where are we to apply the rope? We can't!" They were perplexed.

At that time, when Krishna showed His Universal Form in the assembly of Kurus at Hastinapura, those who were present began to chant in praise of Krishna. Bhīṣma, Drona, Nārada, and Vyāsa were present at that time in the assembly and they began to praise the Lord. Hearing their voices, the blind king Dhṛtarāṣṭra was charmed, and prayed to Krishna: "I can't see You; I am blind. But I hear these great persons chanting Your praises upon seeing Your wonderful form. You can do anything and everything. So for the time being, please remove my blindness; let me see Your figure and color. Let me behold the beauty which they are praising so much. After removing my blindness You may again make me blind." Krishna replied, "It is not necessary for your blindness to be removed. I need only command that you see Me, and you will be able to see Me."

That is the very nature of seeing Him. Our vision of Godhead depends on His will. It is not the eye that can see Him, nor the ear that can hear Him. He is above sense experience. Only by His will may He be seen. He said, "You will see Me," and Dhṛtarāṣṭra saw Him. Although he was blind, still he could see Krishna's divine form. Then what is Krishna? If a deaf man can hear Him and a blind man can see Him, then what is the nature of that divine substance which is Krishna?

Another time, when Arjuna wanted to see the Universal Form of Krishna – the Viśvarūpa – Krishna said: "Yes, Arjuna, see Me!" Arjuna beheld his Universal Form. Krishna asked him, "What do you see?" And Arjuna replied, "I am seeing so many wonderful divine manifestations. It is a wonder of wonders!" So Krishna's sweet will is the basis of everything. We are living in correlation with that absolute power. There is no stability to the environment where we live at present. All importance is on the divine will of Godhead. He is the cause of all causes. From Him this world emanates and by Him it is maintained.

The plane of dedication, however, is far higher than the mundane realm. And we are told that by dedication, by surrender, we can have a direct connection with the center of everything that be. So our advice to the scientists is "Physician, cure thyself! You have come to give so many dazzling models of civilization to the world, but first you should cure yourself fully. What you have come to distribute is all a hoax. The laws of nature, abided by everything that surrounds us, is only the sweet will of the supreme. The laws of nature are not a rigid thing. Their basis is the sweet will of an autocrat. So what you know – that is nothing; it is no knowledge." At any moment, the laws of nature may be changed by the sweet will of the Supreme Autocrat, and another set of rules may completely replace them.

The key to enact the change in our ability to experience reality is in His hands. He may easily say, "O Arjuna, you see this, but I am that." And Arjuna will say, "Yes, now I see that You are that." Everything may be seen in one way by His will and at the next moment that vision of reality may be withdrawn by Him. So the knowledge we can acquire through materialistic education has no value at all. With this realization we should enthusiastically begin the search for Śrī Krishna, Reality the Beautiful.

Krishna is charm Himself. He is the all-charming Absolute. Our innate need is to find sweetness, beauty, *rasa, ānandam*, ecstasy, happiness. Everyone wants this. No one can say "I do not want happiness." No one, from the lowest atheist to the highest theist, can deny this. All will say, "Yes, I want ecstasy; I want sweetness, happiness, peace." This is the common demand in every conceiving unit. From the worst atheist to the greatest theist – wherever there is conception everyone wants peaceful existence. So our direct necessity is with Him, Śrī Krishna, Reality the Beautiful. He is *raso vai sah*: ecstasy, beauty Himself. We must begin our search for that.

Do not lose a moment. Don't waste a minute of your time in wild goose-chasing. Give up everything. *Sarva dharmān parityajya.* Leave it behind. Give up all phases of duty that you are so busily engaged in. It is all worthless. Begin the search for that divine principle who is the creator, the master of everything, and the fulfillment of everything. Search for Him directly. Give up all your so-called obligations and duties in your relative position. They are misconceived, misunderstood from your present defective position. Do not rely on them. Make a direct search for the prime cause from which everything is coming as a miracle. He is the fulfillment of our lives. He is the fulfillment of every atomic existence in all worlds.

We must try to march towards Krishna with His blessings upon our heads. And His agents will give us important help in that direction. Others can do nothing to help us in our inner search; we must take shelter of the saints. We must take shelter of His divine name; it is inseparable from His existence. The sound aspect of divinity can help us a great deal on the way back to Godhead. His holy name is our slogan, our war cry. "Hare Krishna!" With that slogan, we shall march on with His genuine agents. We must follow them and withdraw ourselves from all other possibilities and promises, all so-called prospects of life. They are nothing; they are of no value.

Student: There are many inequities in the world; there is a lot of unfairness, is there not? How can we account for that?

Śrīla Śrīdhar Mahārāj: Fair and unfair are both false. They are just like a dream. One may have a good dream or a bad dream. In either case it is only dreaming. So one should not waste energy to remove the unfair and to increase the fairness. Fair, unfair – it is all false, completely false. In the *Chaitanya-caritāmṛta (Antya-līlā, 4.176)* it is written:

'dvaite' bhadrābhadra-jñāna, saba – 'manodharma'
'ei bhāla, ei manda', – ei saba 'bhrama'

"In the material world, conceptions of good and bad are all mental concoctions. Therefore, saying, 'This is good, this is bad,' is a mistake." The basis of this calculation is false. Our real interest is not there. It is a false scent we are pursuing. Our fulfillment is not to be found in that direction at all.

In this material world there is very little distinction between fairness and unfairness. Everything in this world is based on cheating. Everyone is cheating. There may be cheating of different kinds, but all are cheating. Any fairness or unfairness is an illusion. One may have a good, hopeful dream, or a disastrous dream. But both are dreams. Both are false. And fairness within this world is also false; it is a mental concoction. And what is apparently evil within the relative conception of evil is also false. Why allow ourselves to waste time in a wild goose chase? After all, these relative conceptions of fair and unfair, good and evil, are all false. Whether there is a good hope or a bad hope, all hope within the plane of misconception is based on mental concoction.

Student: But there are so many people that are starving in the world. It seems unfair.

Śrīla Śrīdhar Mahārāj: What to speak of starving, we are in a cave, imprisoned in a cage. That is not desirable for the soul at all. The whole world – suns, stars, moons, oceans, mountains – all are vanishing, and again coming and going. You may be the lord of all you survey, but you are a lord in the cremation ground – a master of the cremation ground, only to deplore, "Oh, everything is passing away. Every second everything is passing away!" In Gray's elegy he wrote,

> **The boast of heraldry, the pomp of power,**
> **And all that beauty, all that wealth e'er gave,**
> **Awaits alike the inevitable hour;**
> **The path of glory leads but to the grave.**

Everything here leads only to the grave and will be finished.

Student: I guess what I want to ask is how we can account for these inequities. I know that you are saying that there is no distinction. But why is there suffering?

Śrīla Śrīdhar Mahārāj: The cause is the misuse of the free will of the *jīva* soul. The misuse of the wealth given to you.

Student: Given by the Supreme Power?

Śrīla Śrīdhar Mahārāj: By the Supreme Power. As a part of a particular potency, you have free will eternally existing within you. And by misuse of your freedom, you have selected to become a king in the mortal world, just as Satan is portrayed in Milton's *Paradise Lost.* He wanted to reign in hell rather than to serve in heaven. The free will – the weak, vulnerable, childlike free will – misused. We came here to be a monarch of all we survey: to reign in hell. Inherent adaptability is an innate feature of the soul. We could have selected service in heaven. Then our desires would have been fulfilled. But we have selected the wrong thing. We have moved in the wrong way. We wanted to be monarch. We could not select slavery in the higher realm. We selected monarchy in hell.

This material world is hell, the soil of affliction. And here we face affliction in variegated ways. These are mainly classified as birth, death, infirmity, and disease. These undesirable things must be there in hell. There is the subtle difference. If you are to live in heaven, then you must live there as a surrendered soul. That is a much higher soil than this. And ultimately we see that to serve in heaven is infinitely better than to reign in hell.

Spiritual Evolution

Question: I want to know more about the position of women in your tradition. Are women allowed to participate in the process of practicing, praying and showing their devotion?

Śrīla Śrīdhar Mahārāj: Who is a woman here may not be a woman there in that higher realm; who is a man here may not be a man there. The body is only a dress. The soul has its mental dress, and according to that, we wear this physical dress, the flesh dress. Sexual identity means the flesh and the mind. In the soul, who will represent which type of sexual identity there, is uncertain at present here in this plane. But women there in the higher realm have a higher prospect – a brighter prospect in the spiritual world.

In the spiritual realm, those souls that are female – who have attained that formation of the soul's realization – hold a better and higher position than men. Here in the plane of exploitation, men hold the better position. But there, in the plane of submission and surrender, the female form of mind is more rewarding than the male's form of mind. The negative aspect of submission is more valuable in connection with Krishna. The supreme positive is

Krishna Himself. And His potency is of a negative nature. We belong to the negative-potency group, not the Master group. The Lord Himself is the possessor of the potency.

Question: You refer to Krishna as Him. Does that mean that Krishna is manifested as a male figure?

Śrīla Śrīdhar Mahārāj: Yes, male. That is, He is the predominating moiety, predominating half of the Absolute. And others are to be predominated by Him. There are two halves of the Absolute Truth: the male half, or predominating moiety, and the female half, or predominated moiety. Positive and negative. It is similar to the concept of the proton and electron, the positive and the negative. The proton is in the center and the electron and innumerable other subatomic particles are like so many planets moving about the center.

Question: Do you believe in the general concept of equality?

Śrīla Śrīdhar Mahārāj: No two things are ever equal, in this world or in the spiritual world. No two things can ever be the same or equal. Everything has its specific characteristic. One atom is different from another atom, one electron is different from another electron. It cannot but be. Everything has its particular differentiated character.

Question: How can you determine whether one thing is superior to another?

Śrīla Śrīdhar Mahārāj: We must judge a thing from the

universal standpoint. If we are to judge a thing, we must judge its quality on the basis of its connection with the Center. That measurement may be made according to the standard of ecstasy, *rasam*, just as gold is the standard for measuring the value of different monetary papers. There may be many currencies – the pound, the ruble, the dollar, the rupee, the yen – but the common standard for determining their value is gold. In the same way, there may be different types of calculation of one's relationship with the Absolute on the basis of *rasa*, ecstasy or divine mellow. *Rasa* is also scientifically divided. *Rasa* is classified in five groups: *śānta*, passive, *dāsya*, servitude, *sakhya*, friendship, *vātsalya*, parenthood, and *mādhura*, consorthood. And then again these groups are classified according to the degree or intensity of *rasa* in each group. Ultimately *rasam*, *ānandam*, happiness – is the common standard by which to judge which religion is higher or lower.

If we want to establish the value of a thing, we must do so by seeing how much of the common requirement it provides. For example, food is a common requirement. We cannot eat dollars in a time of famine. But one who is in possession of food is in a good position. We cannot avoid food. We may not always require dollars, but we must have food. A nation cannot stand without food. That is an indispensable necessity for everyone. In the same way, joy is the innate requirement of every soul, every living thing. And so the position of a particular religious conception may be judged according to the development of *rasa* that may be traced there.

There are different proposals in the religious conceptions of different peoples. There are Christians, Buddhists, Muslims, and Jews. Among those who follow the Vedic doctrines, there are Vaiṣṇavas, Śaṅkarites, and so many others. But if we are to judge the value of different religious conceptions in a comparative study, we must judge their value by three things: *sat, cit,* and *ānandam*. This means we must judge how far a religion is durable, eternal; what is the quality of what is conceived; how far can we conceive of it within the plane of knowledge; and what is its development of *rasa*, *ānandam*. These three things must be there: existence, consciousness, and the food of consciousness – ecstasy, happiness. We are to compare religion on the basis of these three things.

In this way we may ask, "What is the proposal of Islam, Christianity, Judaism, or Buddhism regarding existence, knowledge, and ecstasy, which is the goal of all religion." Christianity, Islam, Vaiṣṇavism – so many religious faiths exist. We are to compare them and then accept what is best. Different adjustments are made by each faith. The different religions of the world are not to be cast away, but there are those for whom each will be – for the present – useful and relevant.

But according to our understanding, Krishna is the personification of ecstasy and beauty. And so the highest religious process for achieving complete ecstasy will be the search for Śrī Krishna, Reality the Beautiful. But how should we search? Through devotion. And what is that? Dedication. What is dedication? Surrender, self-sacrifice –

die to live. And what is living? To live in love, Krishna-*prema*, love divine. The whole picture can be described in two words, Krishna-*prema*. The search for Śrī Krishna is *sambandha jñāna* or understanding our relationship with the object of our fulfillment. Then what is that search, and what is the end of the search? In a few words, in a nutshell, we have described all these things on the title page of our book, *The Search for Śrī Krishna, Reality the Beautiful.*

And this may be understood through the help of Śrī Guru and his grace: it may be explained that the necessity of guru is there, it is universal. To err is human, but not to err is also an inner tendency. Śrī Gurudeva comes to give us relief from our internal trouble. In this way the conception of guru may be developed. The necessity for guru can be inferred from the universal basis of nature which is present around us.

And from there it will gradually move to the absolute. Ultimately the conception of guru will come to Krishna. In this highest sense, Krishna is guru. Who can remove all our doubts, and satisfy all our inquiries? It is Krishna alone. Gradually our faith will develop and take us to the one who can clear all our doubts. We may have doubts upon doubts. One doubt may go and thousands of doubts may come, but guru is one who can clear all our doubts, *bhidyate hṛdaya-granthiś chidyante sarva-saṁśayāḥ (Śrīmad-Bhāgavatam 1.2.21),* who can do away with all the suspicions in our mind; it is he who is full. In this way we must progress. The birth of our faith may be in intellectualism, but its goal is transcendental. The birth of our search and its destination will come to meet together. The birth of faith is from the potency of Krishna, and after moving through the whole of the Infinite it will come again to the potency where we will take our eternal position.

Krishna consciousness means the infinite in the finite: the affectionate connection of the finite with the Infinite helps him to live in infinity. The finite backed by the Infinite may become infinitely resourceful. Our Guru Mahārāj gave the example that if a poor girl marries a prince, although she may have nothing, by her affectionate relationship with the prince, she turns into a princess. So one who has nothing, only a friendly relationship, gets command over everything. This is the nature of Krishna consciousness.

One's resources may increase in that way. Intrinsically, a *jīva* soul is insignificant; it is an infinitesimal point of a point of a point, but by coming in affectionate connection with the Absolute, he gets the facility of all the advantages of a life with the Absolute. Then he or she is in possession of the Whole. We cannot really ascertain anyone's potency or power without considering his relationship with others. Israel is a small country; Russia could conquer it in five minutes, but – America is there. So relationships, connections, and friends must be taken into consideration when understanding the power of a thing.

There is a fable that shows how a small bird was able to disturb and even control the whole ocean. Once, a small bird laid her eggs by the ocean's shore, but the ocean

Garuḍa the carrier of Viṣṇu

carried the eggs away. When the ocean stole her eggs, the bird became angry and asked for them back, but the ocean would not return them. The bird went to her master, that bird went to his master, and in this way they finally went to Garuḍa, the master of all birds. Garuḍa is the servant bird-carrier of Viṣṇu. And Garuḍa came to the aid of that small bird. He threatened the ocean, "If you don't return this little bird's eggs immediately, I shall drink you to the last drop." The ocean had to submit. In this way the unlimited ocean was conquered by a small bird. As the moral of this story, Pandit Viṣṇu Sharma gives this conclusion: "When examining a person, we must consider his friends and the friends of his friends. Without such considerations, we should not try to estimate the power of a particular thing." Because of friendly association, the ocean was conquered. In the same way, by making friendship with the Infinite, one can conquer the Infinite.

Pure Devotion

Once, Bhaktivinoda Ṭhākur had a dream in which he was wandering in the sky chanting the holy name. He came upon the court of Yamarāja, where Yamarāja himself was sitting with Brahmā, Nārada, and others discussing a point from a verse in *Bhagavad-gītā* (9.30):

api cet sudurācāro
bhajate mām ananya-bhāk
sādhur eva sa mantavyaḥ
samyag vyavasito hi saḥ

The generally accepted meaning of this verse is: "Even if one commits the most abominable action, if he is an *ananya-bhāk* devotee who worships Me alone in devotional service which is free from *karma* and *jñāna*, he is to be considered saintly because his endeavors are completely on My behalf and his determination is fixed."

Here, Krishna says, "Whatever he has done, if he is exclusively given to Myself, he should be considered as My devotee. *Samyag vyavasito hi saḥ.* And whatever he is doing is cent percent right." But then the next passage says *kṣipraṁ bhavati dharmātmā:* "very soon he will be a man of righteousness; he will become *dharmātmā* – dutiful."

As Yamarāja, Brahmā, and Nārada discussed this point, a question came up. Krishna says, *bhajate mām ananya-bhāk*, "one who is My exclusive devotee." The question arises, "What is exclusive devotion or *ananya-bhajana*?" Krishna says, "Give up all other religious conceptions and surrender to Me alone": *sarva dharmān parityajya, māṁ ekaṁ śaranaṁ vraja.* That is exclusive devotion. But if one is practicing exclusive devotion, then he is already *dharmātmā*, he is already righteous. How is it then that in the very next verse, Krishna says "soon he becomes *dharmātmā*"? How are we to adjust this? Krishna says:

kṣipram bhavati dharmātmā
śaśvac-chāntiṁ nigacchati
kaunteya pratijānīhi
na me bhaktaḥ praṇaśyati

"He soon becomes righteous *(dharmātmā)* and attains lasting peace. O son of Kuntī, declare it boldly that My devotee never perishes."

This is the general meaning of this verse. Krishna tells Arjuna, "He soon becomes *dharmātmā*. My devotee is never ruined. Go and declare this to the public." Krishna says that after the devotee became *ananya-bhāk* – that is, he gave up all sorts of duties and surrendered to Krishna – then again he will be a dutiful man.

As Brahmā, Nārada, and Yamarāja discussed this point, they saw Bhaktivinoda Ṭhākura walking in the sky and taking the holy name. Then one of them suggested, "There is a pure devotee. He should be able to give the real meaning." Then Bhaktivinoda Ṭhākura was invited in their midst and was asked, "How shall we adjust these points? Krishna has said that this person is an exclusive devotee, that he has renounced all sorts of duties and surrendered to Krishna. And yet, in no time it will be seen that he is very dutiful. How can we understand this?"

Bhaktivinoda Ṭhākura explained that "he quickly becomes righteous" refers not to the exclusive devotee, but to one who considers the exclusive devotee pure in all circumstances. "Even if he performs some abominable act, he is really a *sādhu*, a saint." One who can think of an exclusive devotee in that way will soon become *dharmātmā*. This was Bhaktivinoda Ṭhākura's explanation.

In this way, in my commentary on *Bhagavad-gītā*, I have followed Bhaktivinoda Ṭhākura's explanation. I also saw that it was redundant to say that an *ananya-bhāk* devotee becomes *dharmātmā*. Krishna says that an exclusive devotee should be thought of as a *sādhu*, an honest man. One who says that an exclusive devotee, a surrendered soul to Krishna, should be thought of as pure whatever be his external practices – the man who is making this remark – he becomes righteous. This is the proper conclusion. What he says is cent percent truth. And the next thing Krishna says is that he who can remark in such a way will be purified very soon.

Krishna says that by such appreciation of the exclusive devotee, a person will soon come to his eternal duty and attain eternal peace. "So I ask you, O son of Kuntī, Arjuna, to go and promise in public that My exclusive devotee will never be lost" *(kaunteya pratijānīhi na me bhakta pranāśyati).* Then you will get the benefit of the man whose remark improves his life.

Otherwise, why should Krishna tell Arjuna, "Make a public announcement that My devotee is never ruined." What effect will there be for Arjuna? But one who declares: "an exclusive devotee of Krishna is saintly no matter what he does," soon becomes righteous. If Arjuna declares this, he will become *dharmātmā.* He will get the benefit. So Krishna tells him, "You make this remark. Take a bold step; take a risk and make this remark. Then you will also get that benefit I have described."

Of course, Arjuna is a *parṣada,* an eternal associate of Krishna, but using him as an example, Krishna tells him, "You do it." Arjuna has taken the position of an inquirer independent of his *parṣada* character.

When I was publishing my commentary on *Bhagavad-gītā,* a godbrother once told me, "If you give such an explanation, then in the name of *ananya-bhāk-bhakti,* exclusive devotion, less advanced devotees will take advantage of this. What you are revealing here is a very hidden meaning. It is not meant for the public. It is a confidential point: *api cet su-durācāro bhajate mām ananya-bhāk, sādhur eva:* 'He may be the worst debauchee in his outer life. But if he is *ananya-bhāk,* a surrendered soul, he should be considered a really honest man.' If you explain things according to your interpretation, everyone will say, 'Oh, I am an *ananya-bhāk* devotee,' and they will go on with their debauchery. So please don't express this interpretation of yours so explicitly."

But I published my commentary over this objection because the principle underlying this verse is an important one. One who has surrendered to Krishna is accepted as his own. And just as Krishna has rights over everything and is never a trespasser, so his own man should never be considered a trespasser at any time. This is confirmed elsewhere, in the *Śrīmad-Bhāgavatam*: *ātmā bhūyāya ca kalpate*, "My devotee belongs to Me." So one who works by inspiration from Krishna should never be considered a trespasser. He can enjoy anything on Krishna's behalf if he is really a surrendered soul. He should be considered as Krishna's. He has free access to everything that belongs to Krishna. But some objected, saying, "Don't be so broad in your interpretation. If you do so, then the people at large will do abominable things in the name of pure devotion. They will say, 'Oh, I am Vaiṣṇava. I am *acyuta-gotra*, I am one of Krishna's own men. What is his property is mine. I can enjoy everything.'"

Then of course the question comes, "How do we recognize *ananya-bhāk-bhakti*, exclusive devotion? The real trouble is here. Merely professing that I am a pure devotee won't do. Rather, a real devotee will think, "I am not a real devotee." That will be his understanding, his inner feeling. Exclusive devotion is not a small thing. A genuine devotee thinks, "I can't be an *ananya-bhāk-bhakta*. I have not attained that stage. It is very difficult. Rather I am going away from that." That will be the general tenor of his attitude.

What to speak of lesser devotees, Śrīmatī Rādhārāṇī Herself says, "People associate me with Krishna. They say that I have an illicit connection with Krishna. But what they say is all false. My grief is that I could not give my entire heart to Krishna. I cannot say that I am completely His. My internal trouble is that I could not become wholly His and they falsely think that I am. I have no objection to becoming fully His, even to having an illicit connection with Him; but that I can't become so, this is my great fault." That will be the general attitude of a real *ananya-bhāk-bhakta*.

Just the opposite tendency will come. The fact is that one who has accepted Krishna exclusively has no taste for any other thing, so really he is not *durācāra*; he is not capable of acting in an abominable way. Internally he is always connected with Krishna. In external life he is indifferent. So what he is doing is not done by him. One who acts in that plane of reality may destroy thousands of universes, but does not do anything *(hatvāpi sa imāl lokān na hanti na nibadhyate).* He is acting in the transcendental plane, the *nirguṇa* plane. He is not to be seen in terms of what is good or bad in the calculation of this world. He is absent here.

What is in connection with Krishna is all good; it is *nirguṇa*, transcendental, without material qualities. In this world, truth is a relative thing. "This is true, this is not true, this is mine, this is yours," – what value do these things have? If a devotee steals a flower for Krishna, you may say, "Oh, why are you stealing my flower?" But what is the guarantee that the flower belongs to you? These are different stages of bogus conceptions of reality. A man who has possession of some land declares himself the owner. Then a big landowner comes and says, "You are not the owner. I have real possession of this land. I have allowed you only to use it." But beyond the landowner a king may come and say, "Oh no, this is my land. Your ownership is only relative. I am the ruler of this land. It belongs to me." In this way one relative conception of truth fights with another. And morality stands only on this conception: "this is mine, this is yours."

All these conceptions of ownership are false. All these transactions of morality are false, because they are not in connection with the Supreme Truth. So the devotee's apparent misbehavior is quite the contrary in reality.

> **'dvaite' bhadrābhadra-jñāna, saba –'manodharma'**
> **'ei bhāla, ei manda', – ei saba 'bhrama'**
>
> *Chaitanya-caritāmṛta, Antya-līlā 4.176*

"In the material world, conceptions of good and bad or right and wrong are all mental concoctions. Therefore, saying, 'This is good and this is bad' is all a mistake." So in the deepest plane of reality, the deepest wave of Krishna consciousness is moving, and there so many *jīva* souls are dancing. And that dance is the absolute dance wherein everything surrenders to Krishna in the mood of Vṛndāvana: *sarva dharmān parityajya māṁ ekaṁ.* Everything belongs to Krishna, and for His satisfaction anything and everything can be done. This is the only principle followed by the exclusive devotees without caring for the many relative demands and strictures of this false plane. That is *nirguṇa*, transcendental. In that plane the calculation of false ownership can't be applied. All claims of ownership have no value in Krishna consciousness.

There is another point that may also be considered in this verse. Once, Parāśara Muṇi was crossing a river. A young lady was piloting the boat. As the boat reached the middle of the river, Parāśara suddenly became charmed by that young lady. He proposed that they unite, and they did. As a result of their union, Vedavyāsa was born. Parāśara was already a man of higher sense control. But the time had come for the birth of Vyāsa, and this created a necessity at a particular stage in him. Suddenly he was overwhelmed by lust and united with that lady. From their union came Vyāsadeva, the compiler of all the Vedic scriptures. So this was the determination of the Universal Will. Parāśara is not to be accused or condemned. He is not a party to that. He is an instrument of the Universal Will. We should not consider this an event of lustfulness and criticize Parāśara for his immoral action. He was inspired by some inner will and overpowered by the divine force of the *nirguṇa* will of Krishna. Only then did these things take place.

Therefore Krishna says in the *Bhagavad-gītā* that it is not the action, but the background of the action that is to be considered. That is to be examined, not the action alone. The motive underlying the action, not the *karma*, but the purpose – that is the culprit. Draupadi had five husbands, but not of her own accord. She had to accept the trouble as her duty; she did not do so for the sake of pleasure. So Draupadi should not be held responsible for this; it cannot be said that she is unchaste. She cannot be held responsible for having many husbands. It is said in the *śāstra* that Draupadi or Kuntī may seem to be unchaste, but if you chant their names you will be purified. So the internal meaning of an act, its purpose, should be considered – not the external action.

The higher principle is served not by following ordinary law, but by following some higher law. In that case, the ordinary law is surpassed. One might think a devotee a culprit from the consideration of ordinary law, but from the consideration of a higher law, Krishna has said that if you can appreciate their law-breaking, you will be uplifted.

ajñāyaivaṁ guṇān doṣān
mayādiṣṭān api svakān
dharmān santyajya yaḥ sarvān
māṁ bhajeta sa tu sattamaḥ

Śrīmad-Bhāgavatam 11.11.32

Krishna says, "The rules of the scriptures come from My direction, My order. But if anyone breaks those rules to satisfy Me, he should be considered a better devotee." Sometimes it may be necessary to show even greater loyalty to the king by crossing over the laws of the king. So here God is above law. When we consider the nature of divinity, we must conclude that Krishna is above law. Law is for us. But law may not be applied in His case. He is absolute. When one has actually come in connection with the Absolute, he cannot but ignore the laws meant for ordinary people. Of course, this means in a higher sense. It is not that devotees shall not observe the ordinary laws governing society in the name of devotion. But in the higher sense we have to understand that Krishna is all in all. He is the creator of law and He Himself sometimes breaks the law and especially likes those who are ready to break the law for Him. They are His favorite who are ready to take risks for His service, who are ready to bear the consequence of breaking the law.

This is the nature of Krishna's entire *vraja-līlā*. In Vṛndāvana, all considerations of individual and local interest are sacrificed. In Vṛndāvana, there is the highest self-sacrifice, to the degree that everyone's own particular interest or consideration is sacrificed into fire. Only when you come to that stage of self-sacrifice can you take birth in Vṛndāvana; not before. This is the conclusion of *Bhagavad-gītā*.

sarva-dharmān parityajya
mām ekaṁ śaranaṁ vraja
ahaṁ tvāṁ sarva-pāpebhyo
mokṣayiṣyāmi mā śucaḥ

Krishna says, "You must risk all your prospects, you must risk everything, with no prospects other than Myself. I cannot tolerate the presence of any second entity in your heart. I cannot tolerate that you will come to Me with some consideration. My relation with you must be unconditional. I can't tolerate any other interest in the heart of My devotee. Only one interest, and that is Me. Sacrifice all your so-called interests, all your prospects, everything. Then you can come to meet Me in Vṛndāvana."

The Subjective Bhagavad-gītā

Both Viśvanātha Cakravarti Ṭhākura and Baladeva Vidyābhūṣana have commented on *Bhagavad-gītā*, and Jīva Goswāmī has also given his explanation of different verses. Bhaktivinoda Ṭhākura has given his own explanation, and he has included both Baladeva's and Viśvanātha Cakravarti's commentaries in his Bengali translation of *Bhagavad-gītā*. Śrīdhar Swāmī's commentary was the original one, and Śrī Chaitanya Mahāprabhu had great appreciation for his commentary on *Śrīmad-Bhāgavatam* and *Bhagavad-gītā*.

I have attempted to shed some new light on some verses in *Bhagavad-gītā*. On the basis of what the previous commentators have said, I have shown the further development of *mādhura-rasa* in *Bhagavad-gītā*, and even the paramour relation of *parakīyā-rasa*. When I discussed my explanation with Bhaktivedānta Swāmī Mahārāj, I asked him, "In this place in *Bhagavad-gītā* I have given my interpretation to include *mādhura rasa*. What do you think?" He told me, "What more can be said? Your interpretation is perfectly correct."

Still, it was a new conception I had given there. I found *parakīyā*, the paramour devotion of the *gopīs* for Krishna, represented in the verse *teṣām satata yuktānāṁ...yena mām upayānti te.* Just as *Śrīmad-Bhāgavatam* has four essential verses, there are four essential verses in *Bhagavad-gītā* which contain the very gist, the very substance of the whole ontological conception of *Bhagavad-gītā*.

In *Bhagavad-gītā 10.8,* the first of the four nutshell verses is as follows:

ahaṁ sarvasya prabhavo
mattaḥ sarvaṁ pravartate
iti matvā bhajante māṁ
budhā bhāva-samanvitāḥ

"I am the origin of everything. Everything emanates from Me (including all conceptions of the Absolute Truth and even My own worship). The wise who know this fully worship Me with *bhāva*, deep devotional ecstasy."

Here, Krishna says, *ahaṁ sarvasya prabhavo, mattaḥ sarvaṁ pravartate:* "Everything emanates from Me, including all conceptions of the Absolute Truth." In *Bhāgavatam* the three main conceptions of the absolute are given: Brahman, Paramātmā, and Bhagavān. Brahman means the all-comprehensive aspect of the absolute. Paramātmā means the all-permeating aspect of the absolute, and Bhagavān means the personal conception of the absolute.

In his *Bhakti-Sandarbha*, Jīva Goswāmī has given the real meaning of Bhagavān, the Personality of Godhead. The general meaning of Bhagavān is "one who commands all sorts of potencies." All sorts of potencies are controlled by Him personally. That is the conception of Bhagavān found in Nārāyaṇa of Vaikuṇṭha. But Jīva Goswāmī has given a particularly fine interpretation of Bhagavān. He says that Bhagavān means *bhajanīya sarva-sad-guṇa-viśiṣṭha*: the nature of Bhagavān is such that whatever comes in contact with Him feels a natural serving tendency towards His charming personality. He is endowed with such qualities that everyone is drawn to worship Him, to love Him. He attracts the love of everyone. Everyone wants to serve Him – this is Bhagavān. He is endowed with qualities that attract everyone to serve Him.

I have included this special interpretation of Jīva Goswāmī in my commentary on the above *Bhagavad-gītā* verse. In the *Śrīmad-Bhāgavatam*, three phases of the Absolute Truth have been described (all-comprehensive Brahman, all-pervading Paramātmā, and the all-attractive, absolute person, Bhagavān). I have explained in my commentary that Krishna's statement here *(ahaṁ sarvasya prabhavo)* means: "I am *svayam bhagavān*, the Original Personality of Godhead. I am at the root of all these three conceptions of the absolute. And I am the origin not only of Brahman, the all-comprehensive absolute, and Paramātmā, the all-permeating absolute, but also of Nārāyaṇa, the master of all potencies who commands the respect of everyone. I am the origin of all of Them: I am *svayam bhagavān*."

In this way I have interpreted the meaning of *ahaṁ sarvasya prabhavo*. And in the next line, when Krishna says *mattaḥ sarvaṁ pravartate*, here we must concentrate more finely. Krishna says *sarvaṁ pravartate*, "everything comes from Me." With this Krishna is saying: "Even worship of Me comes from Me. I reveal it first. I Myself worship Myself. I do this as *guru*, as My finer potency. This potency is nothing but Myself. And My finest potency is Rādhārānī. Through My potency I worship Myself. Every movement begins from Me; even My own worship, My own service is begun by Me, in My role as *guru*. I reveal that to the public so that you will properly worship Me. For this reason *guru* is called Bhagavān, for he is nondifferent from Me *(ācāryaṁ māṁ vijānīyāṁ)*."

The finest potency of Bhagavān is Rādhārāṇī. So *guru* in the highest sense, as well as service in the highest sense, is represented in Śrīmatī Rādhārāṇī. Next, Krishna says, "Those who know this will worship Me: *iti matvā bhajante mām*." Those who understand this conception that Rādhārāṇī serves Him in the highest way, will serve Krishna in subjugation to Her. That is *rādhā-dāsyam*, the divine service of Śrī Rādhā. And it is with this understanding that a worshiper will come to worship Krishna.

In my interpretation, I have taken it that this is Krishna's intent when He says, *iti matvā bhajante mām*: "Knowing this, they worship Me." He means "those who know that My worship comes from Me, and that My finest potency worships Me best, will worship Me under the direction of My finest potency." Here we find the importance of *rādhā-dāsyam*, the service of Śrī Rādhā, the highest goal of the followers of Rūpa Goswāmī, the *rūpānuga-gauḍiya-*

sampradāya. Here, Krishna is saying, "Knowing that it is My finest potency that worships Me best, one will worship Me under the direction of My first-class worshiper (Śrī Rādhā). With this idea one will always worship Me under the guidance of My finest *śakti*, Śrīmatī Rādhārāṇī, or Her representation, Śrī Gurudeva. In this way, they will always worship Me under their direction, and never as a direct worshiper." This is the meaning of *iti matvā bhajante mām.*

Then Krishna says *budhā bhāva-samanvitaḥ*. Here, *budhā* means those of fine theistic intellect *(sumedhasaḥ).* In *Bhāgavatam* it is said that those of fine theistic intellect will be able to appreciate this *(yajanti hi sumedhasaḥ).* Fine theistic intelligence is the outcome of good fortune which comes from above *(sukṛti)*; it is not self-acquired. That fine intellectual inner direction and guidance can only come from the *nirguṇa* or transcendental plane. *Budhā* here means "one who has a direct connection with the *nirguṇa* or transcendental plane." His intelligence doesn't come from this *māyic* quarter; rather it springs from the spiritual platform. Only such a person can appreciate these subtle points. This is said in *Bhāgavatam*:

kṛṣṇa-varṇaṁ tviṣākṛṣṇaṁ
sāṅgopāṅgāstra-pārṣadam
yajñaiḥ saṅkīrtana-prāyair
yajanti hi su-medhasaḥ

"Those who are of fine theistic intellect *(sumedhasaḥ)* will worship Śrī Chaitanya Mahāprabhu in *saṅkīrtana*, not others."

So this verse from *Bhagavad-gītā* means, "One whose devotion is the product of the *nirguṇa* wave, whose faith is not collected from this world of misunderstanding, shall worship me through *rādhā-dāsyam.*" Here *bhāva-samanvitaḥ* means *rāga-samanvitaḥ* – that is, they worship Krishna with *anurāga*, love. Their affinity for Krishna, their devotion to Him, is not governed by rules; it does not spring from strictly following the scriptural rules, but from *bhāva*, inner inspiration. This worship is called *rāga-marga*, the path of spontaneous attraction.

Scriptural rules involve calculations of loss and gain. But worship which is *bhāva samanvitaḥ* is not drawn from any consideration of loss and gain; it flows naturally through love and attraction for Krishna. It is *jñāna-śunya-bhakti*, free from calculation, free from profit and loss: *jñāna-karmādyanāvṛtam.*

The next of the four essential verses which contain the entire message of *Bhagavad-gītā* is as follows *(10.9):*

mac-cittā mad-gata-prāṇā
bodhayantaḥ parasparam
kathayantaś ca māṁ nityaṁ
tuṣyanti ca ramanti ca

"The hearts and minds of My devotees are always filled with Me, and they are forever experiencing pleasure and ecstasy in talking about Me."

Here, Krishna says, "I am in their hearts, in their thinking *(mac-cittā mad-gata-prāṇā).* Their whole life, their entire energy is spent for Me, utilized for Me. Their *prāṇā-śakti*, their life-energy, is also fully devoted for My cause. Internally they are always thinking about Me and devoting their whole energy for Me, and externally they talk about Me to enhance their mutual understanding *(bodhayantaḥ parasparam).* They love to talk about Me with one another; they talk about nothing else. In private life, and in public life also, they love to talk about Me, and nothing else. I am the only subject of their discussions *(kathayantaś ca māṁ nityaṁ).* Whatever they do, wherever they are – everywhere, I am the subject of their talk."

And next Krishna says, "In this they find great satisfaction *(tuṣyanti ca ramanti ca).*" The internal meaning of *tuṣyanti ca ramanti ca* is as follows. Here two levels of devotees are described. Up to *vātsalya-rasa*, or the parental mellow of devotion, Krishna's devotees are feeling great satisfaction *(tuṣyanti).* And above this is the higher kind of satisfaction *(ramanti)* experienced in the *mādhura-rasa.* Just as a wife and husband enjoy a particular kind of connection, Krishna's devotees feel ecstasy *(ramanti)* in His connection, simply by talking about Him. Here the *āchāryas* have agreed that the word *ramanti* indicates consorthood, and that devotees in consorthood can experience the very deep connection of husband and wife in relation to Krishna. In the company of Krishna they feel the ecstasy of consorthood, *ramanti ca.* They also feel that ecstasy even when they are only talking about Krishna. This meaning of the word *ramanti* has been explained in different places by Viśvanātha, Baladeva, Bhaktivinoda Ṭhākura, and is also admitted even by Śaṅkarāchārya, who agrees that the word *ramanti* indicates consorthood.

Then there is the next nutshell verse of *Bhagavad-gītā (10.10):*

teṣām satata-yuktānāṁ
bhajatāṁ prīti-pūrvakam
dadāmi buddhi-yogaṁ taṁ
yena mām upayānti te

"To those who constantly worship Me with devotion, I give the intelligence by which they can come to Me."

This is the ordinary meaning of this verse, but there is a deeper meaning. Here, Krishna says: "Those persons who are continuously engaged in Me without interruption *(satata-yuktānāṁ)*, who are always in Me, who are connected with Me, who serve Me with great love and respect with their heart, *dadāmi buddhi-yogaṁ taṁ* – I inspire them with the intelligence by which they will come to Me. They will come to Me in a closer connection." But I found that this is redundant. Krishna has already said *satata-yuktānāṁ*, "Their devotion is continuous; they are always there in My connection." If they are already in connection with Krishna, then we must ask why He would again say, "They will come to Me."

Krishna has already said that these devotees talk only of Him, think only of Him, take pleasure in Him, and are always engaged in His service. He says, "They are always connected with Me without interruption, and they are serving Me with heart felt love." They are already serving with heart-felt love, and then Krishna says, "I shall give them the inspiration by which they will come to Me" *(mām upayānti te)*.

This is redundant. It has already been said that they are connected to Krishna; how is it that again they will "come to Him"? How is Krishna's statement "they come to Me" to be harmonized? So I found a deeper meaning to the words *mām upayānti te*. I took here the word *upayānti*, which ordinarily means "they come", to indicate *upapati*, or "paramour." So *upayānti* – "they come to Me" – means they consider Krishna as *upapati*, as a paramour.

In society there is the lawful husband, or *pati*, and there is the paramour, or *upapati*. In Vṛndāvana, Krishna is not considered by the *gopīs* as their lawfully married husband, but as master, as the Lord of their hearts.

Here Krishna says, "I inspire those who are constantly engaged in devotional service to come to Me." Which devotees does Krishna here inspire? Those who are *ramanti*, the highest group of devotees, those who are related to him in consorthood, in full *rasa* – *mukhya rasa*. Krishna says here, "I inspire them to come to Me, considering Me as paramour, *upapati*. Here Krishna says *bhajatām prīti-pūrvakam*: this means *prema*, which is generally found in *mādhura rasa*, consorthood. So the real meaning of this verse is that Krishna inspires those who are in consorthood to come to Him, seeing Him as paramour, *upapati*. And how do they come to Him? He inspires them to come to Him without any consideration of social and scriptural demands. And so, inspired by Him from within, crossing the line of scriptural and social regulations, and even deceiving their own husbands, the *gopīs* are united with Krishna in paramour consorthood (*parakīyā*).

Krishna's position is absolute, and He relishes more the devotion of those who can cross everything for Him. And He inspires his devotees from within with this message: "Externally you have to fulfill social and scriptural demands, but My position is over and above the scriptures. My position is above whatever the social laws and scriptural laws tell you to do. I am above the *Vedas* and everything else. The *Vedas* are My instructions for the ordinary people. Their instructions are meant for those who are deviated from Me. Society is also under the guidance of those instructions which were given to the fallen. But My connection with everything is intrinsic; it is independent of the laws of scripture and society. I do not require recognition from anyone. My connection with everything is the constant in all equations. It can never be avoided. So you must neglect all the demands from your previous life's connections and come to Me. You have no freedom to do anything else. When your devotional nature will come to demand you to come to Me, you are not free. Your heart must come towards Me."

That is *upapati*, paramour devotion. The devotion of Vṛndāvana, *vṛndāvana bhajana*, means paramour devotion: *yena māṁ upayānti te.* So here Krishna says that to those who are *ramanti*, who are already inclined to come in connection with Him in consorthood as husband and wife, He gives some special feeling and inspiration within their hearts, and they shall come to Him as *upapati*, as paramours. Here Krishna is saying, in effect, "This paramour devotion is so great that it crosses the rules of both society and scripture. It is independent of everything. Connection with Me is independent of everything that you can conceive. It is most innate and natural. It does not require any scriptural or any social sanction. You may live in society showing formal respect to scriptural and social convention, but from your inner heart of hearts you are Mine. That is *yena māṁ upayānti te*, the special instruction or nature or insight I give to these devotees."

In other words, these devotees do not allow a second *pati* or husband to come between them and Krishna. They cannot tolerate the interpolation of any second thing, even if it involves social laws or scriptural regulations. Their devotion is so high that all the *Vedas* are searching after this idea, this divine position.

āsām aho caraṇa-reṇu-juṣām ahaṁ syāṁ
vṛndāvane kim api gulma-latauṣadhīnām
yā dustyajaṁ sva-janam ārya-pathaṁ ca hitvā
bhejur mukunda-padavīṁ śrutibhir vimṛgyām
Śrīmad-Bhāgavatam 10.47.61

"Although the most exalted devotion of the *gopīs* is only hinted at in the *Vedas*, I can now understand their most exalted position. O when shall I take birth as a creeper in Vṛndāvana, so that I can take the dust of the lotus feet of the *gopīs* upon my head? Those great souls gave up society, friendship, love, their relatives – and even the Vedic principles – to take shelter of the holy lotus feet of Krishna."

Here, one thing should be mentioned: *parakīyā-bhāva* has a broader application. It does not only mean paramour devotion. This feeling of crossing scriptural and social rules for an "unsanctioned" relationship is found not only in *mādhura-rasa* or consorthood. *Parakīyā* literally means "belonging to another." *Vātsalya-rasa*, parental affection, and *sakhya-rasa*, friendship, are also infused with the sentiments of *parakīyā*. This is the method of love for those who follow *rāga-marga*.

In the case of Yaśodā, *parakīyā* takes the following form: Yaśodā says, "Some people say that Krishna is not my son. They say that he is Devaki's son!" This feeling enhances her heart's affection towards Krishna, for then she thinks, "I could lose Him at any moment." This idea draws more intense affection towards Krishna. It increases the affection of her service.

In *sakhya-rasa*, the sentiments of *parakīyā* are also found. "Some say Krishna has come from Mathurā and he may again go to Mathurā. He does not belong to us; he is not exclusively our friend." This apprehension also fills the minds of the cowherd boys, and they become anxious, thinking, "We may lose Him at any time." So that sentiment makes friendly service towards Him more intense. In this way, the whole sentiment in Vṛndāvana is *parakīyā*.

In the mood of servanthood, or *dāsya-rasa* also, there is some sentiment like that. Devotees feel, "Some say that Krishna comes from Mathurā, that He is the son of Vasudeva. He is here only for a while; He is not an ordinary man like us." This idea is more or less current in Vṛndāvana. So *parakīyā* is not only found in *mādhura-rasa*; Krishna may capture all with that sentiment.

Parakīyā is a very special thing in *mādhura-rasa*. Its

speciality is that in *mādhura-rasa* it is more objectionable both to the scriptures and to society. But for the *gopīs* it is not objectionable. In *mādhura-rasa* they have to cross over the directions of both the *Vedas* and society – they must take that great risk. In other *rasas* there is only the fear that "We may not have Krishna permanently, He may go away, He does not belong among us..." This suspicion increases the intensity of their service, but in *mādhura-rasa*, they must cross the positive directions of the *Veda* and society. They must go against these authorities, as if to take the risk of committing sin. This is the special feature of *parakīyā* in *mādhura-rasa*, so there the intensity of devotion is in its highest condition. So the inspiration towards *parakīyā (yena māṁ upayānti te)* that Krishna discusses here with special reference to those who are *ramanti*, who are connected to Him in consorthood, is also present in all the servitors in Vṛndāvana.

Finally, we come to the last of the four nutshell verses *Bhagavad-gītā 10.11:*

teṣām evānukampārtham
aham ajñāna-jaṁ tamaḥ
naśayāmy ātma-bhāvastho
jñāna-dīpena bhāsvatā

Krishna says: "To show them special mercy, I enter their hearts and destroy their ignorance with the lamp of knowledge."

The inner meaning of this verse is more difficult to draw out. The words *teṣām evānukampārtham* may be interpreted in two ways. The external interpretation is that Krishna favors His devotees, and the internal explanation is that Krishna is saying, "I want their favor: I aspire after the favor of the devotees of the highest order." As in *Bhāgavatam (10.82.44),* Krishna says:

mayi bhaktir hi bhūtānām
amṛtatvāya kalpate
diṣṭyā yad āsīn mat-sneho
bhavatīnāṁ mad-āpanaḥ

"My dear *gopīs,* everyone considers themselves fortunate if they possess devotion for Me, and by that they achieve an eternal life of nectar. But I must admit that I consider Myself most fortunate because I have come in touch with the wonderful affection found in your hearts."

Still the paradox is that Krishna seems to say that after such grief and continued engagement with Krishna, then He gives these higher devotees pure knowledge, and by that knowledge they get salvation by attaining Brahman. That is the point of argument made by the followers of Śaṅkarāchārya. But I have taken it in another direction.

Jñāna-dīpena is a troublesome expression – "I enlighten them with knowledge" – so I have given another interpretation: When the pangs of separation felt by Krishna's devotees comes to its extreme stage, Krishna suddenly comes and shows Himself. For example, Śacīdevī feels extreme separation when she cooks for Nimai, and then by His mercy she can see clearly that Nimai has come and taken *prasādam.* Similarly in Vṛndāvana, when the pangs of separation reach

their highest degree, then suddenly the devotees can see that "Krishna is here in our company." So when Krishna says that out of His mercy He appears and removes their ignorance, their *ajñāna*, he means that when the devotees are experiencing separation from Him, He appears before them and removes the darkness they feel from separation. Out of His mercy, He gives them sustenance. And when that sort of medicine has been applied, they can go on further. In Vṛndāvana, when His devotees felt separation, sometimes He had to come and to show His friends, "I am amongst you. I have not left you." This is what is meant by dispelling darkness with the light of divine knowledge: *jñāna-dīpena bhāsvatā*. Here the word ignorance or *ajñāna* means *jñāna-śunya-bhakti*, knowledge-free devotion. Devotees do not think that they are part and parcel of the *līlā*, the pastimes of the Supreme God. No; their devotion is free from such calculation. It is *jñāna-śunya-bhakti*: most innocent.

Here Krishna is saying, "I can't tolerate the pangs of separation felt by My devotees. I must run towards them and show them, 'I am here, My mother. You see? I am here taking food.'" Sometimes Śacīdevī prepares food for the Deity, and after offering it, she sees that it is all gone. At that time, she thinks, "Was this a dream? I saw Nimai. He was taking *prasāda*, and of course nothing was left in the pot. But Nimai has gone long ago. But then who has taken this *prasāda*? What was it I saw? Was it a dream, or has some dog taken the food? Or is it that I forgot, I have not cooked today? Perhaps I did not give the *bhoga* to the Bāla Gopāla deity. What did I do?"

In this way, Śacī is confused. This may be seen as her *ajñāna*, her "ignorance." Then Śrī Chaitanya sends some devotee to her, saying, "You tell all this to my mother: on those days when such things occur I actually go there; I take food from her hand. It is not a dream. Remind My mother of this and console her. Tell her that I come to her and I take her cooked *prasādam*. Remind her that this has occurred."

So this is the meaning of the fourth nutshell verse from *Bhagavad-gītā*: by His mercy Krishna removes the darkness of separation from His devotees. And those that remind us of Krishna, and thus remove the darkness born of separation from Him, are the real humanitarians. They are distributing the highest cure. The *gopīs* tell Krishna: "We are suffering from this pang that is created by You. But the messages about Your pastimes give us life and sustenance. We are eager to hear this, and then we may feel that we are getting our life back. There is no other medicine but Your assurance and consolation: that alone can save us from these pangs of the burning heart." This is their statement in *Śrīmad-Bhāgavatam (10.31.9):*

tava kathāmṛtaṁ tapta-jīvanaṁ
kavibhir īḍitaṁ kalmaṣāpaham
śravaṇa-maṅgalaṁ śrīmad-ātataṁ
bhuvi gṛṇanti ye bhuridā janāḥ

"O Krishna, we are always suffering in this world, but just hearing the nectar of Your words and pastimes gives us life and as a by-product it removes all of our sinful reactions.

This sort of hearing is all-auspicious and fills us with spiritual wealth. Those who deliver this message of Godhead are doing the highest relief work for human society and are actually the greatest humanitarians."

The Gāyatrī Mantra

The meaning of the *brahma gāyatrī* must bring us to the conclusion of *Śrīmad-Bhāgavatam*. The *gāyatrī mantra* and the *Śrīmad-Bhāgavatam* are one and the same. It is the very gist of the *Vedānta-sūtra*. *Śrīmad-Bhāgavatam* is the elaborate commentary of *gāyatrī*:

artho 'yaṁ brahma-sūtrāṇāṁ
bhāratārtha-vinirṇayaḥ
gāyatrī-bhāṣya-rupo 'sau
vedārtha-paribṛṁhitaḥ

Garuḍa Purāṇa

The meaning of the *gāyatrī mantra* must be in the line of *Śrīmad-Bhāgavatam*. If we analyze how this is possible, we shall uncover the steps leading the *gāyatrī mantra* to the *Śrīmad-Bhāgavatam*.

What is the meaning of *gāyatrī*? The word *gāyatrī* is a combination of two Sanskrit words: *gānat* (what is sung) and *trāyate* (gives deliverance). This means, "A kind of song by which we can get our salvation, relief, emancipation." *Gāyatrī* is known as *veda-mātā*, the mother of the

Vedas. And Gāyatrī has produced the whole Veda. If we examine the Vedic conclusion from its most condensed aphorism to its most extensive expression, we shall find that it begins with *oṁkara*: the Vedic syllable *oṁ*. That truth is expressed as the *gāyatrī mantra*, then it appears in the form of the *Vedas*, and then as the *Vedānta-sūtra*. Finally, the Vedic conclusion is given its fullest expression in the *Śrīmad-Bhāgavatam*. Since the meaning, the purpose of Vedic knowledge progresses in this line, the *gāyatrī mantra* must contain within it the meaning of *Śrīmad-Bhāgavatam* – that is, that the Krishna conception of Godhead is the highest.

This must be the meaning of the *gāyatrī mantra*, but the problem is how to extract *Śrīmad-Bhāgavatam* – the Krishna conception – from within the womb of *gāyatrī*. I heard that Jīva Goswāmī has given such an interpretation, but I could not find where it is written. I heard that he has given the meaning of *gāyatrī* leading to Krishna consciousness. Anyhow, the tendency awakened in me to draw the meaning to the Krishna conception.

The general meaning of *gāyatrī* is "that song which grants liberation." Liberation must have some positive meaning. Liberation means not freedom from the negative side, but positive attainment. This is the definition given in *Śrīmad-Bhāgavatam: muktir hitvānyathā rūpaṁ svarūpena vyavaṣthitiḥ* – unless and until we attain the highest possible positive position, real *mukti*, real salvation, has not been effected. Mere withdrawal from the negative plane cannot be called liberation. Hegel has said that the object of our life is self-determination. We must determine our normal function in the organic whole – not mere emancipation from the negative side, but participation in a positive function in the domain of service. This is considered to be the highest attainment of life. This is the real meaning of *gāyatrī.*

The word *gāyatrī* comes from two Sanskrit roots: *gānat* and *trāyate. Trāyate* means positive attainment to the final stage *(sva-rūpena vyavasṭhitiḥ).* And *gānat* means not mere sound, but musical sound. That musical sound which grants us the highest positive deliverance indicates the *saṅkīrtana* of Śrī Chaitanya Mahāprabhu and the flute-song of Śrī Krishna.

The purport of the *brahma-gāyatrī mantra* is as follows: The first word is *oṁ. Oṁ* is the seed mantra which contains everything within it. The next word is *bhūr. Bhūr* is where we are, Bhū-loka, the world of our experience. The next word is *bhuvaḥ.* Bhuvar-loka is the world of mental acquisition. It is the support, the background of our experience. Our present position of experience is the effect of our mental acquisition. That we are here in the world of experience is not an accident; we have acquired this position by our previous *karma.* The physical sphere, this present world of experience, is only the product, the outcome of our previous mental impulses. And the subtle world of previous *karma,* the mental sphere, is known as Bhuvarloka.

The next word in the mantra is *svaḥ.* Above Bhuvarloka is Sva-loka. The mental world (Bhuvarloka) means acceptance and rejection: what to do and what not to do – "I like this, I don't like that." Sva-loka, however, is the plane of decision, the world of intelligence (Buddhiloka). Our intelligence tells us, "You may like this, but don't do that, for then you will be the loser." That plane, the plane of reason, is known as Sva-loka. In this way, this material world is composed of three general layers, *bhūr*, the physical world, *bhuvaḥ*, the mental world, and *svah*, the intellectual world.

Of course, a more detailed analysis will reveal seven layers: Bhūr, Bhuvaḥ, Svaḥ, Mahā, Jana, Tapa, and Satyaloka. This has been dealt with in detail by Sanātana Goswāmī in his *Bṛhad-Bhāgavatāmṛtam*. Here, these seven strata have been summarized in three planes of existence: physical, mental, and intellectual. And these three planes of experience have been summarized in a word, *tat*.

The next word in the *brahma-gāyatrī*, is *savitur*. *Savitur* generally means *sūrya*, the sun. And the sun means, figuratively, that which shows or illuminates; that by which we can see. The three gross and subtle strata within this world are shown to us by a particular thing, *savitur*. What is that? The soul. Actually, the world is not shown to us by the sun, but by the soul. What really gives us perception and allows us to see gross things? It is not actually the sun that helps us see; we see with the help of the soul. This is found in *Bhagavad-gītā (yathā prakāśayaty ekaḥ kṛtsnaṁ lokam imaṁ raviḥ)*. The soul reveals this world to us just as the sun does. The sun can show color to our eyes, the ear can reveal the sound world, and the hand can reveal the touch world. But really in the center is the soul. It is the soul who gives light to this world, who gives us an understanding of the environment, the world of perception. All perception is possible only because of the soul. Here, the word *savitur*, which generally means sun, can only mean soul, for the soul, like the sun, shows us everything.

All seven strata of our existence – represented by *bhūr*, the physical plane, *bhuvaḥ*, the mental plane, and *svaḥ*, the intellectual plane – have here been reduced to one entity: *tat* – "that." "That" is shown by the sun which in this context indicates the soul. Here soul means individual soul. The individual soul is the cause of his world. Not that the mind is in the world, but the world is in the mind. Berkeley has said that the world is in the mind. Here it is being expressed that everything is seen with the help of the sun. If there is no sun, everything is dark – nothing can be seen. So without light, nothing can be seen. And in a higher sense, light means the soul. The soul is the subject and the soul's object is the seven planes of experience within this world.

The next word in the *gāyatrī mantra* is *vareṇyaṁ*. *Vareṇyaṁ* means *pūjya*: worshipable, venerable. This indicates that although within this plane – the objective world – the soul is the subject, there is another domain which is to be venerated and worshiped by the soul. That is the Supersoul area.

That worshipable plane of transcendental existence is known as *bhargo*. *Bhargo* means the supersubjective area, the area of the Supersoul. This is mentioned in the first verse of *Śrīmad-Bhāgavatam: dhāmnā svena sadā nirasta-kuhakaṁ satyaṁ paraṁ dhīmahi.* Śrīla Vyāsadeva says that here he is going to deal with another world whose pristine glory is so great that by its own ray, all misconceptions are brushed aside. The subject is the soul, and its object is all these worlds of experience. And the supersubject is the venerable area which is superior to the subject, the soul – that is the supersubjective area.

The word *bhargo* means "more subtle than the soul," and "holding a more important position than the soul." So this means the Supersoul, the Paramātmā. In general, of course, the word *bhargo* ordinarily means light. Just as an X-ray can show us what the ordinary eye cannot see, *bhargo* is *svarūpa-śakti*: higher, more powerful light that can reveal the soul. And that energy – *bhargo* – belongs to whom? It belongs to *deva*. What is the meaning of the word *deva*? *Deva* means "who is beautiful and playful", that is, Śrī Krishna: Reality the Beautiful. He is not a nondifferentiated substance, but is full of *līlā*, pastimes. *Deva* means pastimes and beauty combined, and this means Krishna.

His domain is *bhargo*, brilliant, and it is *vareṇyaṁ*, to be venerated by the *jīva* soul. What is the nature of the *svarūpa-śakti*? It is the *vaibhava*, the extension of Śrīmatī Rādhārāṇī. She holds the full service responsibility and the energy to serve Krishna. *Bhargo* is no less than the *vaibhava*, the extended body of Śrīmatī Rādhārāṇī, which contains everything for the service of Krishna. *Bhargo* represents Mahābhāva, the predominated moiety, and *deva*, Krishna, is Rasarāja, the predominating moiety.

In the *gāyatrī mantra*, we are requested, *bhargo deva*sya *dhīmahi*: "come meditate." What sort of meditation is possible in that plane of dedication? Not abstract meditation, but service cultivation, *kṛṣṇānuśilanam. Dhīmahi* means "to participate in the spontaneous flow, the current of devotion in Vṛndāvana." And what will be the result *(dhiyo yo naḥ pracodayāt)*? The capacity of our cultivation will be increased. As we serve, a greater capacity and willingness to serve will be given to us in remuneration – just as interest is added to capital in the bank *(dāsa kari' vetan more deha prema-dhana)*. In this way, our dedicating principle will be increased again and again. *Dhīmahi* means *ārādhana*, worship. It cannot but be explained in terms of *ārādhana, pūjā, sevā* – worship, adoration, loving service. The word *dhī* is derived from the word *buddhi*, which generally means that which we cultivate with the help of our intelligence. But here, *dhī* is a reference to that venerable intelligence which descends into this plane to help us cultivate service. So *dhīmahi* does not mean abstract meditation, but devotional service. This is the underlying meaning of the *gāyatrī mantra*.

Gāyatrī, the song for deliverance, also means *saṅkīrtana. Kīrtana* is also sung, and it also improves us towards the highest goal. The *saṅkīrtana* of Śrī Chaitanya Mahāprabhu also reinstates us in our highest serving position. So *brahma-gāyatrī* in connection with Mahāprabhu comes to mean Krishna-*kīrtana*. Then it reaches Vṛndāvana and the flute-*kīrtana*. And when we enter Vṛndāvana, we shall find that the sweet sound of Krishna's flute helps to engage all the Lord's servants in their respective duties. When the flute is sounded, the *gopīs* and others are adjusted in their respective duties. At night, the *gopīs*, hearing the sound of the flute, will run to the Yamunā, thinking, "Oh, Krishna is there." And when Yaśodā hears the song of Krishna's flute, she thinks, "My son is there. He is coming home soon." In this way, the sound of the flute engages all the servants of the Lord in their respective positions and inspires them to be mindful of their service.

In my Sanskrit commentary on the *gāyatrī mantra*, I have written *dhīrārādhanam eva nānyaditi tad rādhā-padaṁ dhīmahi:* All other services are represented fully in Rādhikā. Like branches they are all part of Her. *Mādhura rasa* is the chief or *mukhya-rasa*, the combination of all *rasas*. Śrīmatī Rādhārāṇī is Mahābhāva – She represents the entire serving attitude.

The flute-song of Śrī Krishna, expressed as the *gāyatrī mantra*, is reminding us and engaging us in our service. And what is our service? Our service must be to surrender ourselves in the service of Śrīmatī Rādhārāṇī – to accept the suggestion of Rādhārāṇī. The *gāyatrī mantra* will excite us to be mindful about Śrīmatī Rādhārāṇī's lotus feet, to obey Her orders. She is mainly representing the whole serving area. So to try to engage ourselves in Her service, under Her order – to accept Her direction and to obey Her – that is the service of Śrī Rādhā. In this way, the meaning of the *gāyatrī mantra* has been drawn to *rādhā-dāsyam*, self-determination *(svarūpena vyavasthitiḥ)*.

In the meantime, the partial representations in *vātsalya* and *sakhya rasa* are also part and parcel of the original mellow of conjugal love, *mādhura rasa*. The *vātsalya rasa* devotee will serve Nanda and Yaśodā, the *sakhya rasa* devotee will serve Śrīdāma and Sudāma, but ultimately, the whole system in one conception is included in Rādhārāṇī.

Rādhā-dāsyam, the service of Śrīmatī Rādhārāṇī, is the ultimate meaning to be extracted from the *gāyatrī mantra*. That is the supreme end of our life. It cannot but be so. *Śrīmad-Bhāgavatam* is the ultimate or full-fledged theism to be extracted from the *Vedas*, *Upaniṣads*, and so many scriptures. All the revealed truth rises to its acme, to its highest position, in the conception given by *Śrīmad-Bhāgavatam*. And *Śrīmad-Bhāgavatam* teaches us that the highest realization, self-determination, is to be found in the service of Śrīmatī Rādhārāṇī – that under her guidance we may serve Śrī Krishna. We aspire for a direct connection with Her service.

What, then, is the inner meaning and purport of the word *bhargo? Bhargo vai vṛṣabhānuja-ātmā-vibhava-eka-ārādhana-śrī-pūram. Bhānu* means the sun, or "who shows us by light." Rādhārāṇī is the daughter of Vṛṣabhānu. So I selected the word *bhānu*. To represent her personal extended self, I have given the word *vaibhava*. *Vaibhava* means, "what comes out," or "extended self." *Prābhava* is the central representation and *vaibhava* is the outer extension. The very gist of *svarūpa-śakti* is Śrīmatī Rādhārāṇī, and the whole *svarūpa-śakti* is Her extended self. The town of Her beautiful service, that is, the country, the abode of Her beautiful service is the whole *svarūpa-śakti*.

Just as rays of light extend from the sun, the whole internal potency is an extension of Mahābhāva, Śrī Rādhikā. She has developed Herself into such a beautiful area of brilliance, of internal energy, and thereby She serves Her Lord. All these necessary things have sprung from Her. To help Her in serving Her Lord, they all come out. When the entire internal energy is condensed in a concise form, it is Mahābhāva, Rādhārāṇī. And when Rādhārāṇī wants to serve, She extends Herself in limitless different ways. And with some contribution from Baladeva and Yogamāyā, the whole spiritual world, including Vṛndāvana, Mathurā, and Vaikuṇṭha, evolves to assist Śrīmatī Rādhārāṇī in the service of Śrī Krishna.

In this way, I have drawn out *rādhā-dāsyam*, the service of Śrīmatī Rādhārāṇī as the meaning of the *gāyatrī mantra* and have tried to represent it in Sanskrit verse.

Gaura Haribol!

About the Author

His Divine Grace Śrīla Bhakti Rakṣak Śrīdhar Deva-Goswāmī Mahārāj was born in Hāpānīya, West Bengal, India in 1895. In 1927 he was initiated as a disciple of Śrīla Prabhupāda Bhaktisiddhānta Saraswatī Ṭhākura, the founder-*āchārya* of the Gauḍiya Maṭh and foremost Vaiṣṇava scholar of the twentieth century. Śrīla Śrīdhar Mahārāj's scriptural genius, penetrating realizations, and strict practice of the devotional principles of Gauḍiya Vaiṣṇavism were soon recognized by Śrīla Bhaktisiddhānta Saraswatī, who in 1930 awarded him the renounced order of *sannyāsa.* He was named *Bhakti Rakṣak Śrīdhar*, or "guardian of devotion," after the original *Bhāgavatam* commentator Śrīdhar Swāmīpāda.

Bhaktisiddhānta Saraswatī saw him as especially fit to protect the Gauḍiya Vaiṣṇava line from misrepresentation. After reading one of his Sanskrit compositions glorifying Bhaktivinoda Ṭhākura, Bhaktisiddhānta Saraswatī remarked, "Now I am satisfied that, after I leave, there will be at least one man who can represent my conclusions *(bhakti-siddhānta).*"

After the passing of Śrīla Bhaktisiddhānta Saraswatī, Śrīla Śrīdhar Mahārāj established his own temple, Śrī Chaitanya Sāraswat Maṭh, on the banks of the sacred Ganges in Nabadwīpa Dhāma, the holy land of Śrī Chaitanya Mahāprabhu. Having deeply assimilated the teachings of Śrī Chaitanya, he began composing original texts. His first work, *Śrī Śrī Prapanna-jīvanāmṛtam*, was a comprehensive scriptural study of surrender. His Divine Grace composed numerous songs, prayers, and commentaries. Among these important works are his commentary on Bhaktivinoda Ṭhākura's *Śaraṇagati*, Bengali translations of *Bhagavad-gītā* and *Bhakti-rasāmṛta-sindhu*, and his own original Sanskrit poem summarizing *Chaitanya-līlā*, *Prema-dhāma-deva-stotram.* An outstanding contribution to the Rupānuga Gauḍiya Sampradāya is his commentary on the *gāyatrī mantra* in the line of *Śrīmad-Bhāgavatam.*

Original works in English translation include: *The Hidden Treasure of the Sweet Absolute (Bhagavad-gītā)* and *Life-Nectar of the Surrendered Souls: Positive and Progressive Immortality (Śrī Śrī Prapanna-jīvanāmṛtam).*

At an advanced age in his fully matured stage of realization, Śrīla Śrīdhar Mahārāj spoke extensively on the teachings of Śrīla Saraswatī Ṭhākura, Bhaktivinoda Ṭhākura, and the great predecessor *āchārya*s. Some of his English language publications are: *The Search for Śrī Krishna: Reality the Beautiful, Śrī Guru and His Grace, The Golden Volcano of Divine Love, Loving Search for the Lost Servant, Subjective Evolution of Consciousness: The Play of the Sweet Absolute, Śrī Śrī Prapanna-jivanāmṛtam: Life Nectar* *of the Surrendered Souls, Heart and Halo, Holy Engagement, The Golden Staircase, Home Comfort, Inner Fulfillment and Sermons of The Guardian of Devotion I – IV.*

After his passing in 1988, he was succeeded by his dear-most beloved disciple and appointed successor, Śrīla Bhakti Sundar Govinda Dev-Goswāmī Mahārāj.

Main International Centres

For a full list and further information: www.scsmath.com

India

International Headquarters:
Sri Chaitanya Saraswat Math
Sri Chaitanya Saraswat Math Road,
Kolerganj, Post Office: Nabadwip
District: Nadia,
West Bengal, Pin 741302, India
http://scsmath.com

Sree Chaitanya Saraswata
Krishnanushilana Sangha,
487 Dum Dum Park (Opposite Tank 3),
Kolkata, Pin 700055, West Bengal

Sree Chaitanya Saraswata
Krishnanushilana Sangha,
Kaikhali, Chiriamore,
P.O. Airport, Kolkata, Pin 700052,
West Bengal, India

Sri Chaitanya Saraswat Ashram,
P.O. and Village Hapaniya,
District of Burdwan,
West Bengal, India

Sri Chaitanya Sridhar Govinda Seva Ashram
Village of Bamunpara, P.O. Khanpur
District of Burdwan, West Bengal, India

Sri Chaitanya Saraswat Math
Bidhava Ashram Road, Gaur Batsahi
Puri, Pin 752001, Orissa, India
Tel: +91 9937479070

Srila Sridhar Swami Seva Ashram
Dasbisa, P.O. Govardhan
District of Mathura, Pin 281502
Uttar Pradesh, India
Tel: +91 7247889384

Sri Chaitanya Saraswat Math & Mission
113 Seva Kunja, Vrindavan
District of Mathura, Pin 281121
Uttar Pradesh, India
Tel: +91 9761876054

Sri Chaitanya Saraswat Math
Hayder Para, New Pal Para,
155 Netaji Sarani, Siliguri, Pin 734006,
West Bengal, India
Tel: +91 9748906907

Sree Chaitanya Saraswata
Krishnanushilana Sangha,
Garbhabas (Ekachakra Dham),
Post Office: Birchandrapur,
District: Birbhum,
West Bengal, PIN 731245

Srila Sridhar Govinda Sundar Bhakti Yoga
Cultural Centre, Flat 6, (Top floor),
House 2394, Tilak St. (Behind Imperial
Cinema), Chuna Mandi, Pahar Ganj,
New Delhi 110055
Mobile: +91 9810309511

U.S.A.

Sri Chaitanya Saraswat Seva Ashram
2900 North Rodeo Gulch Road
Soquel, CA 95073, U.S.A.
Tel: (831) 462-4712
www.SevaAshram.com/

Sri Chaitanya Saraswat Seva Ashram
269 E. Saint James Street
San Jose, CA 95112, U.S.A
Tel: (650) 550-8573

Sri Chaitanya Saraswat Mission
745 South 700 East
Salt Lake City, UT, 84102
http://scsmission.com

Hawaii

Sri Chaitanya Sridhar Govinda Mission
16251 Haleakala Hwy., Kula, Maui,
Hawaii 96790, USA.
Tel: 808-878-6821
http://www.krsna.cc

Canada

Sri Chaitanya Saraswat Sridhar Asan,
#29 9955 140 Street,
Surrey, V3T 4M4, Canada.
Tel: 604.953.0280
http://scsmath-canada.com

Mexico

Mérida
Sri Chaitanya Saraswati Sridhar Govinda
Sevashram de México, A.R.
Calle 69-B, No. 537, Fracc. Santa Isabel
Kanasín, Yucatán c.p. 97370, Mexico
Tel: (52-999) 982-8444

Guadalajara
Sri Chaitanya Saraswati Sridhar Govinda
Sevashram de México, A.R.
Reforma No. 864, Sector Hidalgo
Guadalajara, Jalisco, c.p. 44280, Mexico
Tel: (52-33) 3826-9613

Monterrey
Sri Chaitanya Saraswati Sridhar Govinda
Sevashram de México, A.R.
Diego de Montemayor 629,
Centro, Monterrey, N. L., c.p. 64720
Tel: (52-81) 8057-1097

Tijuana
Sri Chaitanya Saraswat Sridhar Govinda
Sevashram de México, A.R.
Avenida de las Rosas 9
Fraccionamiento del Prado
Tijuana, B. C., c.p. 22440
Tel: (52-664) 608-9154

Celaya
Sri Chaitanya Saraswati Sridhar Govinda
Sevashram de México, A.R.
Potasio # 224, Fracc. Zona de Oro II
Celaya, Gto., c.p. 38030
Tel: (52-461) 614-9001

Veracruz
Sri Chaitanya Saraswat Math de Veracruz, A.R.,
Juan de Dios Peza 157
(entre Ignacio de la Llave y Negrete)
Veracruz, Veracruz, c.p. 91700
Tel: (52-229) 955 0941

Orizaba
Sri Chaitanya Saraswati Sridhar Govinda
Sevashram de México, A.R.
Colón Poniente 213 - Interior 7
Col. Centro, c.p. 094300, Orizaba, Ver., Mexico
Tel: (52-272) 725-6828

México D.F.
Sri Chaitanya Saraswati Sridhar Govinda
Sevashram de México, A.R.
Fernando Villalpando No. 100 - Int. 103
Col. Guadalupe Inn,
Delegacion Alvaro Obregon, c.p. 01020
Mexico City Tel: (52-55) 5097-0533

Sri Chaitanya Saraswati Sridhar Govinda
Sevashram de México, A.R.
Calle Z edif. 40 Int 22 Col. U H Alianza
Popular Revolucionaria,
Delegacion Coyoacan, c.p. 04800
Mexico City Tel: (52-55) 5677 8315

Morelia
Sri Chaitanya Saraswati Sridhar Govinda
Sevashram de México, A.R.
Joaquín Rivadeneyra No. 50
Col. Jardines de Guadalupe
Morelia, Mich., c.p. 58140
Tel: (52-443) 275-2875

Ticul
Sri Chaitanya Saraswati Sridhar Govinda
Sevashram de México, A.R.
Carretera Ticul - Chapab, Km 1.4,
Ticul, Yucatán, Mexico.

Europe

England
Sri Chaitanya Saraswat Math
466 Green Street
London E13 9DB, U.K.
Tel: (0208) 552-3551
http://scsmathlondon.org

Sri Chaitanya Saraswat Math,
Bhakti Yoga Institute,
Greville House, Hazelmere Close,
Feltham, Middlesex TW14 9PX, U.K.
Tel: +44 2088909525

Republic of Ireland
Sri Chaitanya Saraswat Sangha
Attn: Brian Timoney
(Ballinamore, Co. Leitrim)
Tel: 071 9645661

14 Parkside, Wexford Town,
County Wexford, Ireland
Tel: 086 2626 475

Italy
Villa Govinda Ashram
Via Regondino, 5
23887 Olgiate Molgora (LC)
Fraz. Regondino Rosso, Italy
www.VillaGovinda.org
Tel: [+39] 039 9274445

Sri Chaitanya Saraswat Math Rome
VedaVita Yoga Studio
Via di San Michele, 12
00153 Roma. Italy
Tel. +39 06 69371556

Malta
The Lotus Room Yoga Centre Malta
Tel (mobile): [+356] 9986 7015

Netherlands
Sri Chaitanya Saraswati Sridhar Ashram
Azorenweg 80
1339 VP Almere, Netherlands
Tel: 036 53 28150

Hungary
Sri Chaitanya Saraswat Math
Andras Novak
Nagybányai út 52. H-1025 Budapest
Hungary Tel: (361) 3980295

Sri Chaitanya Saraswat Seva Ashram
Endre Szepesi – Ananda Vardhan d.
H-1223 Budapest
Muvelodes utca 17/B, Hungary

Turkey
Sri Govinda Math Yoga Centre
Abdullah Cevdet sokak
No 33/8, Cankaya 06690
Ankara, Turkey
Tel: 090 312 4415857 & 090 312 440 88 82
www.yogamerkezi.org

Ukraine
Kiev, Harmatnaya st. 26/2,
"Rostok" Palace of Culture
Tel: +38 (044) 496-18-91
+38 (067) 464-18-94

Sri Chaitanya Saraswat Seva Ashram
11/4 Panfilovsev Street
Zaporozhya, 69000, Ukraine
Tel: (0612) 33-42-14

Asia

Thailand
Sri Chaitanya Sridhar Govinda Ashram
79/23 Mooban Worabodin
Soi Watsadet
Pattumthani-Rangsit Road, Pattumthani,
Bangkok, Thailand
Tel: +66 819 095 917

Malaysia
Sri Chaitanya Sridhar Govinda Seva
Ashram, Sitiawan.
Tel: 017-5862817 / 012-5012804

Sri Chaitanya Saraswat Sadhu Sangam Klang,
No 14, Lorong Bendahara 46A,
Taman Mewah Baru,
41200 Klang, Selangor, Malaysia.
Tel: +60 3-51616721

Sri Chaitanya Sridhar Govinda Seva Ashram,
Petaling Jaya Service Centre,
No: 13 Jalan 18/16, Taman Kanagapuram,
46000 Petaling Jaya, Selangor, Malaysia.
Tel: +60-1-63386130

Singapore
Sri Chaitanya Saraswat Math Singapore
and Gokul Vegetarian Restaurant
19 and 21, Upper Dickson Road,
Singapore 207478
Tel: 63439018
Mobile: 90236341 and 91856613

Philippines
Srila Sridhar Swami Seva Ashram
c/o Gokulananda Prabhu
23 Ruby St., Casimiro Townhouse,
Talon Uno, Las Pinas City,
Metro Manila, Zip code 1747,
Tel: 800-1340

Sri Chaitanya Saraswat Math,
Philippines Branch (Ishani Devi Dasi)
Lot 15 Block 8, Woodbridge Subdivision,
Poblacion, Pandi., Bulacan,
Philippines, 3014
Tel: +63 92031 63750
http://philippines.scsmath.org

South Pacific

Australia
Sri Govinda Dham
P.O. Box 72, Uki, via Murwillumbah
N.S.W. 2484, Australia.
PTel: (0266) 795541

Sri Chaitanya Saraswat Ashram
14 Brian St, Brinsmead
Cairns, QLD, Australia 4870
Tel: 0432 054 048

Made in the USA
Monee, IL
22 December 2020

55302420R00105